Hey Larry + Debbie,

It's been a while, I hope I
will get to see you sometime. I
hope this book is a blessing
to you.

David Jarrett

# PROSPEROUS AND SUCCESSFUL

PURSUING GOD'S PLAN FOR YOUR LIFE

DAVID JANARO

WESTBOW
PRESS®
A DIVISION OF THOMAS NELSON
& ZONDERVAN

WestBow Press books may be ordered through booksellers or by contacting:

WestBow Press
A Division of Thomas Nelson & Zondervan
1663 Liberty Drive
Bloomington, IN 47403
www.westbowpress.com
1 (866) 928-1240

Because of the dynamic nature of the Internet, any web addresses or links contained in this book may have changed since publication and may no longer be valid. The views expressed in this work are solely those of the author and do not necessarily reflect the views of the publisher, and the publisher hereby disclaims any responsibility for them.

Any people depicted in stock imagery provided by Getty Images are models, and such images are being used for illustrative purposes only. Certain stock imagery © Getty Images.

Unless otherwise noted, all Scripture is taken from The Holy Bible, New International Version®, NIV®. Copyright © 1973, 1978, 1984, 2011 by Biblica, Inc.® Used by permission of Zondervan. All rights reserved worldwide. www. Zondervan.com. The "NIV" and "New International Version" are trademarks registered in the United States Patent and Trademark Office by Biblica, Inc.®

Scripture quotations marked ESV® are from The Holy Bible, English Standard Version®. Copyright © 2001 by Crossway Bibles, a publishing ministry of Good News Publishers. Used by permission.

Scripture quotations marked NASB are from the New American Standard Bible®. Copyright © 1960, 1962, 1963, 1968, 1971, 1972, 1973, 1975, 1977, 1995 by the Lockman Foundation. Used by permission. (www.Lockman.org)

ISBN: 978-1-9736-7193-0 (sc)
ISBN: 978-1-9736-7195-4 (hc)
ISBN: 978-1-9736-7194-7 (e)

Library of Congress Control Number: 2019912815

Print information available on the last page.

WestBow Press rev. date: 09/13/2019

To Cheryl, Micah, and Josiah
My continual reminders of God's goodness

# CONTENTS

# INTRODUCTION

Keep this Book of the Law always on your lips; meditate on
it day and night, so that you may be careful to do everything
written in it. Then you will be prosperous and successful.

—Joshua 1:8

The first person to hear the Joshua 1:8 promise faced enormous
pressures. Joshua was the newly appointed leader of a swarm of
runaway slaves preparing for war. Only a narrow, meandering river
separated him from some of the fiercest and well-fortified people
in the ancient world. Countless men, women, and children were
looking to him for leadership and strength. They had little military
experience and no sophisticated weapons.

At that moment, God approached Joshua with special instructions
that came with a guarantee of prosperity and success. Think about
what an all-knowing God could have said. He could have shared
winning strategies for siege warfare that no one else would think of
for centuries. He could have told Joshua about the most important
psychological principles for leading untrained soldiers into a fierce
battle. He could have revealed the weakest points in the city's walls
and the best time to catch the guards in the middle of a shift change.
God did none of that. Instead, he informed Joshua that he already
had what he needed to guide him at this crucial moment. All the
essential principles for success were explained in a new book Moses

had recently finished writing under God's guidance. "Follow this book," God said, "and you will be prosperous and successful."

Yes, *that* book. The one accused of promoting slavery and genocide. The backward book said to oppose science and progress, the usual suspect for charges of sexism, racism, and homophobia. A book containing lists of strange and archaic sounding laws, genealogies, and silly stories. Joshua could easily have responded, "Really? Is that all you've got? I need military strategy, and you're offering me stories about Adam and Eve and talking snakes, and so forth? That just might make for an interesting bedtime story for my children, but now?"

Although the book Joshua held in his hands was a recent publication, it could easily seem just as irrelevant and unrelated to the daily challenges of life then as it does to us, living thirty-five hundred years later. And yet, the Bible claims throughout that it is the uniquely qualified guide to a prosperous and successful life. The promise appears again in different forms in the Psalms, Prophets, and the teachings of Jesus and Paul.[1] The Joshua 1:8 promise is for us as well. Admittedly, the Bible is not the most obvious source of information for navigating the complexities of twenty-first-century life. But not everything that is true is immediately obvious.

The rest of the events recorded in the book of Joshua show how the promise became a reality in Joshua's life. Although from a human standpoint, there was no reason to think that following God's teaching would lead to success, it certainly did. God told Joshua to use an unusual military strategy to conquer the city of Jericho. It involved marching around the city, again and again, and blowing trumpets (not exactly a tried and true method of siege warfare). And yet, when Joshua and the Israelites obeyed, God gave them the victory (Joshua 6). In the next battle, the Israelites assumed they would have little trouble defeating the much smaller town of Ai. However, because they failed to follow God's instructions, they faced humiliating defeat (Joshua 7).

At this point, you may wonder if Joshua was even a real person. Perhaps even more surprising is the claim that God actually gave this promise to Joshua. You may be thinking, *God actually spoke to a real person named Joshua? And we know this? And this is actually relevant to my life?* These are all great questions to ask, because following Joshua 1:8 is no simple task. The verse calls on us to think continuously about an admittedly strange-sounding ancient book, telling us to "meditate on it day and night." Not only that, but it says we are actually supposed to "do everything written in it." It's hard to imagine a higher level of commitment. Anyone would be foolish to follow this verse without valid reasons for doing so.

And yet, what if it is true? I believe the Joshua 1:8 promise is true, and I believe it is the key to a successful life. My goal is to lead you to consider believing this as well and to learn how to use the Bible to guide you to success in every area of life. So this isn't another success book. This is an endorsement and guide to another success book, the only necessary one ever written and the ultimate resource for life.

## How the Bible Can Be the Ultimate Resource for Life

Is the Bible's promise in Joshua 1:8 true? In order to find the answer, I think it is best to start with a more modest question. Is it even possible that it is true? For if it is not even possible, then there is no reason to go any further. If it is at least possible, then it is worth your time to evaluate the evidence and to at least consider the claims the Bible is making.

First, the Bible not only claims to be the ultimate guide to prosperity and success; it also claims to have the necessary ingredients to deliver on such a promise. The Bible claims to be the very words of God. According to the opening words of the book of Joshua, "After the death of Moses the servant of the LORD, the LORD said to Joshua son of Nun, Moses' aide: 'Moses my servant'" (Joshua 1:1).

The author of Joshua is telling us that everything in the eight verses that follow is an actual quote of the God who made the heavens and the earth. This includes the literally God-given secret to a successful life found in the eighth verse. If there is even a possibility that the words of the Bible have a divine origin, then it is also possible that the Bible is the definitive book on success. If God really told Joshua that the key to success in life is meditating on and carefully doing everything taught in the Bible, then we have every reason to believe that the Bible genuinely is the ultimate resource for life.

According to the Bible, God created us. He knows exactly how we function and what our purpose is. He knows everything about us, even the number of hairs on our head (Matthew 10:30). He has known everything about billions of people who have lived over thousands of years. And he loves us. He has infinite wisdom and understanding about everything we need to know to find success and prosperity. So, if he has informed us that the Bible is the authoritative guide to a successful life, then we can be sure it is.

The question, of course, is whether God really gave the promise in Joshua 1:8. Can we trust anything written in the Bible? The Bible itself tells us that the struggle to recognize God's voice is as old as Adam and Eve. When the serpent tempted Eve in the garden of Eden, his opening line was, "Did God really say, 'You must not eat from any tree in the garden?'" (Genesis 3:1). If you struggle to believe that God has spoken and that his words are recorded in the Bible, you are in good company. However, the Bible is written in a way that addresses those concerns. God does not simply ask you to blindly believe.

## Jesus on Success

If we had nothing more than what the book of Joshua claims about the Bible, then we'd have very little reason to take it seriously. Perhaps Joshua was simply looking for a way to get political support from the people he was leading. It's not hard to imagine that he would consider convincing the ancient people under his command that God spoke to him and gave him a divine mandate to lead. The story would make for great propaganda and would solidify the nation's support. Maybe he made the whole thing up. Maybe he didn't even exist but was a character created later in history to encourage Israelites to join the military. Maybe the rest of the Bible is nothing more than a collection of writings used to control the ignorant and get them to support the interests of the ruling class. Do we have any reason for believing that the book of Joshua should not be explained away along one of these lines?

Yes, we do have more than simply what the book of Joshua claims. The strongest support for the Bible comes from a Jewish rabbi who lived many centuries after Joshua. Many believe that he is the Messiah, or Savior, a person predicted in the Book of the Law that God gave to Joshua. We know him by the name Jesus, and his teaching ministry and life on earth provide corroboration to Joshua's story. He is the key to trusting that the Bible is an authentic success book with a divine guarantee. With Jesus, we have a man who testified that he himself was God. He provided sufficient lines of evidence to support this claim. He told us that the Bible is the very Word of God. He repeated the Joshua 1:8 promise in various ways, telling us that the key to a prosperous and successful life is available to all who will meditate on and carefully obey the teachings in the Bible.

For example, Jesus concluded his famous Sermon on the Mount by saying, "Therefore everyone who hears these words of mine and puts them into practice is like a wise man who built his house on the rock. The rain came down, the streams rose, and the winds blew and beat against that house; yet it did not fall because it had its foundation on the rock" (Matthew 7:24–25).

Here, Jesus substituted the words in Joshua 1:8, "Keep this book of the Law always on your lips," with "everyone who hears these words of mine." Jesus used the word *hear* to mean something like "pay close attention to." Next, Jesus added the qualification "and puts them into practice," just like the command in Joshua 1:8 to "be careful to do everything written in it." As Joshua 1:8 concluded with the promise of prosperity and success, Jesus assured his followers that they will be "like a wise man who built his house on the rock." Jesus used the image of a man's house standing as a metaphor for someone who has a successful life. His house stood, even when a great storm came with strong winds beating against it.

Jesus also contrasted the wise man with a foolish man who built his house on sand. The foolish man's house fell, representing someone who failed in life. The reason, according to Jesus, is that he did not put the lessons of the Sermon on the Mount into practice (Matthew 7:26–27). For Jesus, following the Sermon on the Mount is the same thing as following the Bible, including the Book of the Law that God told Joshua to follow.

In Joshua's time, the Book of the Law would have been only the first five books of today's Bible; the rest was written later. Jesus referred to the Book of the Law and the additional books of the Bible in the Sermon on the Mount when he said, "Do not think that I have come to abolish the Law or the Prophets. I have not come to abolish them but to fulfill them." He went on to add, "whoever practices and teaches these commands will be called great in the kingdom of heaven" (Matthew 5:17–19). Just like the Joshua 1:8 promise, the Sermon on the Mount represents Jesus's call to carefully obey everything written in the Bible.

Jesus even referred to the Bible specifically as "the Word of God" at different times in his ministry. For example, in Mark 7:10, Jesus quoted one of the Ten Commandments to the religious leaders: "For Moses said, 'Honor your father and mother.'" Jesus pointed out that certain traditions they had created were contrary to God's command. He explained this by stating, "Thus you nullify the word of God by your tradition" (Mark 7:10–13). Jesus called the Bible the Word of God and also cited it as an authority over human tradition.

For Jesus, identifying the Bible as the Word of God means that whatever it commands or promises is authoritative and trustworthy. When Jesus faced temptation in the wilderness, he quoted repeatedly from the Bible, introducing each passage with the phrase, "It is written" (Luke 4:4, 8, 12). Jesus assumed that if it is written in the Bible, then no other supporting argument is necessary, only obedience. He was saying that you can trust its words and must do what it says.

Think of Jesus as the ultimate witness, with the Bible on trial. The prosecution lists reason after reason why the Bible can't be trusted. It challenges the credibility of every step in the process that would be necessary for the Bible to be a divine success book. It presents arguments against everything from the existence of God to the possibility of God speaking to people. The prosecution also questions whether the words we have now are accurate and unaltered records, even if God were behind the original writings. After hours of presentations, the jurors' heads are spinning. At first, the defense seems to have little to offer to counter the various charges.

However, at this moment, Jesus takes the stand. He is the defense team's star witness. He was actually present when the Bible was written. He can vouch for the Bible's authenticity. You do not need to believe that the Bible is God's Word to see the historical evidence that Jesus made these claims and supported them. I believe any reasonable jury would be persuaded by the evidence, and I hope that you will be as well. God invites you to look at the evidence, even if you begin with a fair amount of skepticism, because he wants you to know the truth.

I believe that Jesus is the foundation for why you should believe that the claims of the Bible are true, but I will give additional ways to verify that this is so. The Bible itself functions as a type of witness to its own credibility. It does this by carefully recording prophecies that have come to pass, pointing to historical evidence that can be verified by outside sources, and giving practical teachings on various topics that our experiences confirm.

In this book, I intend to accomplish two objectives. I want to help grow your confidence that the Bible is true and that it is the ultimate resource for life. I will begin in chapter 1 by clarifying what the Bible means by "success." What exactly is the Bible promising in Joshua 1:8 that I am asking you to believe? Indeed, not only to believe, but on which to place all your hope for a truly successful life. Chapter 2 will focus specifically on why you can trust that this promise is true. In subsequent chapters, I will explain how we know the Bible is true and show you how to use it effectively to obtain the Joshua 1:8 promise in your life.

---

1.  Examples include Deuteronomy 30:9–14, Psalm 1:1–3, Psalm 119:105, Isaiah 5:24, Matthew 7:24–27, Matthew 11:28–30, John 13:17, 2 Timothy 3:16, James 1:25, and 2 Peter 1:19.

# PART I
## FOUNDATIONS FOR PURSUING SUCCESS

# CHAPTER 1

# DEFINING SUCCESS

> What good will it be for a man if he gains the
> whole world, yet forfeits his soul?
>
> —Matthew 16:26

I once coached my three-year-old son's soccer team. I use the word *coached* loosely. Soccer skills were irrelevant to the position. A professional cat herder would have more qualifications for coaching the team than a former World Cup soccer player. My first objective was getting the kids to kick the ball. The only other task was getting the kids to kick the ball in the right direction!

Inevitably, I experienced failures in the second category. The ball would roll behind the swarm of kicking feet and flailing arms. A kid would break away from the pack, eyes gleaming. He would go to kick the ball the wrong way. You could see it in his face. This was his moment, his chance to break away from all the commotion, race down the field unhindered, and impress everyone with the big kick and goal. While he zoned in on the big opportunity in front of him, all the other voices around him suddenly seemed distant. Paying attention to them might break his concentration on the ball and the goal ahead.

With shouts of "Wrong way!" and "Turn around!" raining

down on the field from myself and other parents, he was having the moment of his life. Until, that is, the ball went through the goal and into the net. As he turned around, he did not find the anticipated applause and celebration but hanging heads and uncomfortable silence.

Being prosperous and successful in life requires pursuing the right goal. No matter how good you may feel about how things are going, if you aren't going in the right direction, it's all a waste. In soccer, going the right direction is more difficult than going in the wrong direction. When you dribble the ball toward the right goal, your opponents will chase you and kick the ball away from you. Go in the wrong direction, and the defenders, not wanting to impede your error, will run away from you. It's easier to go the wrong way, but what's the point? You avoid the difficulties but arrive at the wrong destination.

Before you can consider whether the Bible really is the ultimate guide to success, you need to know the direction it is pointing. The Bible is a book that identifies various wrong goals for life. At the same time, it carefully defines and argues for one right goal, acknowledging that it is often not an easy one to pursue. It describes why the one right goal is worth it, resulting in peace, joy, and success. Finally, it gives all the necessary and detailed instructions on how to pursue the correct goal and be prosperous and successful while doing so.

## The Right Goal

The Bible identifies glorifying God as the correct goal for life. "Whatever you do, do it all for the glory of God" (1 Corinthians 10:31). This is not a popular goal. If there were a "goal of life" vending machine with a row of buttons identifying different options for people to choose from, the "Do Everything for God's Glory" button would not be pushed very often. It doesn't sound like there's anything in it for me. What about what I want? What about *my* glory? Doing everything for someone else's glory sounds like a losing proposition, not a path to success. A recent survey found that

86 percent of Americans agree with the statement "To be fulfilled in life, you should pursue the things you desire most."[1] Seems like common sense, right?

Pursuing God's glory as the goal of your life is counterintuitive. That is probably why Jesus needed to emphasize it frequently in his teaching ministry. Jesus told his disciples, "For whoever wants to save their life will lose it, but whoever loses their life for me will find it" (Matthew 16:25). Why make such a confusing statement? Jesus acknowledged that what the Bible calls on us to do goes against the normal way of thinking. He was also saying that living for God's glory isn't simply giving up on any hope to have joy in your life. It's not as if the Bible has nothing to offer but to call on you to endlessly suffer and give up on one dream after another so you can please some taskmaster god. No, Jesus was saying that practicing self-denial to live for God's glory is worth it. You will end up finding your life. Living for anything else would actually be losing your life.

One of Jesus's most popular promises is "Come to me, all you who are weary and burdened, and I will give you rest" (Matthew 11:28). These words are another variation of the promise of success in life. We all want rest from the many burdens that weigh us down. It's not hard to see why this promise is encouraging to many of Jesus's followers.

But contrast this with what Jesus said to his disciples in Luke 9:23 (ESV): "If anyone would come after me, let him deny himself and take up his cross daily and follow me." Now this is not one of Jesus's most popular sayings. It sounds at odds with his other promise for rest.

Furthermore, his call to take up a cross probably sounded harsher in biblical times than it does to us. Today, we have a positive view of the cross. We see it on top of churches, displayed prominently in great works of art, and adorned with gold and diamonds in jewelry. Many stores even sell crosses made from chocolate around Easter each year. The cross is now a comforting candy for children. But that was not the case in Jesus's day.

Jesus gave this statement before his Crucifixion and resurrection.

There was nothing positive about a cross at all. When the disciples heard the word *cross,* they probably thought back to the first time they were coming into Jerusalem on one of the main roads and saw several naked, dead men left for days on crosses as a way of reminding all Jews to be terrified of breaking Roman law. The cross represented excruciating pain and oppression. (The word *excruciating* comes from the word *crucifixion.*) Who would ever volunteer to "take up his cross"?

How could Jesus give a hopeful promise for the weary and burdened on one occasion and urge gruesome sacrifice on the other? Was he simply in a good mood one day, giving out promises of rest, and then in a foul mood the next, calling on people to pick up a cross? Actually, I think these two verses are one and the same, just stated in different ways.

Notice that Matthew 11:28 is not just a promise but a promise with a command. Jesus begins with the command "Come to me." But what does it mean to come to Jesus? The popular understanding of this phrase is that we come to Jesus with our problems. We share them with him in prayer, asking him to lighten the load for us. But that is not really what Jesus is talking about. Coming to Jesus includes that idea but encompasses so much more.

As in every verse in the Bible, we need to interpret the passages in their context. Jesus does not leave it up to us to guess at what he means by "Come to me." He tells us in the next verse, "Take my yoke upon you and learn from me" (Matthew 11:29). Coming to Jesus means learning his teachings. A yoke kept two oxen heading in the same direction as the farmer plowed his fields. Taking Jesus's yoke upon you means to tie yourself to Jesus and his teachings—to go in the same direction he does. We "learn from" him and then do what he says.

Taking on his yoke is doing exactly what Jesus called for in Luke 9:23: "If anyone would come after me." There, Jesus explained that coming to him involves denying yourself. The same is true in Matthew 11:28–29. Coming to Jesus involves taking a yoke that keeps you going in the same direction as Jesus, instead of whatever direction you want to go in. It means following him by living the way he lived and obeying his teachings.

The most important teaching for us to follow, according to Jesus, is to live for God's glory as the goal of life. You may be tempted to ask, "But what's in it for me? Who is this God that I should sacrifice all my wants and desires for his glory?" Jesus was not saying living for God's glory will be easy. He was saying that it will be worth it. It is the only goal worth living for. To be successful, you can't simply pursue the things you desire most. That is the easy path. Instead, you must pursue God's glory most.

Jesus often spoke about the contrast between following the difficult path that leads to success and the easy path that leads to destruction. He demonstrated his concern for getting people to consider the right goal in life with this question: "What good will it be for a man if he gains the whole world, yet forfeits his soul?" (Matthew 16:26). He gave a sober warning when he said, "Enter through the narrow gate. For wide is the gate and broad is the road that leads to destruction, and many enter through it. But small is the gate and narrow the road that leads to life, and only a few find it" (Matthew 7:13–14).

Jesus was essentially saying that going the wrong way in life seems right and is easy, but we should not be deceived. There are all sorts of popular paths that are dead ends. They lead to great difficulties in life. In contrast, going toward the right goal is difficult initially. However, this "narrow road" leads to something that is worth it. This is what Jesus called "rest" in Matthew 11:28.

Jesus emphasized that glorifying God is the proper goal of life. He said it when he was asked to identify the most important commandment. "Love the Lord your God," Jesus replied, "with all your heart and with all your soul and with all your mind" (Matthew 22:37).

In the Bible, love is not simply an emotional desire to have a close relationship with someone. It involves sacrificing one's own interests for the interests of another. Love means doing. For example, in John 3:16, the Bible tells us that "God so loved the world that he gave his one and only Son." God loved by giving up what was his to benefit others. According to Jesus, the most important command in the Bible is to love God, to have a willingness and desire to sacrifice anything, including our thoughts, dreams, and comfort, if it will contribute to God's glory. By the way, this command does not appear for the first time in the teachings of Jesus. Rather, Jesus is quoting from Deuteronomy 6:5, part of the Book of the Law that God told Joshua was the key to being prosperous and successful.

Jesus also described the goal of life in Matthew 6:33: "But seek first his kingdom and his righteousness, and all these things will be given to you as well." It's even in the Lord's Prayer, found in Matthew 6:9–13. Jesus told his disciples, "This, then is how you should pray." Then he gave the most famous prayer in the Bible. It begins, "Our Father which art in heaven, Hallowed by thy name" (Matthew 6:9 KJV). Notice that Jesus said that the first thing we should ask for in our prayers is that God's name be "hallowed," meaning sanctified or set apart from all other names.

The first thing we pray for is a reflection of what we desire most. It betrays what is most pressing on our minds. If my greatest desire is financial provision, that is what I will want to ask for first. Jesus included financial provision in his model prayer when he added later on, "Give us this day our daily bread," but he reserved the opening of the prayer for a plea for God's name to be hallowed.

## Why This Goal?

One of the great mistakes people make in reading the Bible is to view it as a series of stories and rules, where the main point of each story is to reinforce the moral lessons stated directly in the rules. "Do this," "Don't do that," "Don't even think about doing—." If the Bible was reduced to a series of "Thou shalt not" commandments, it would truly be an oppressive bore.

One example of viewing the Bible this way is exemplified in a recent bestselling book, *The Year of Living Biblically: One Man's Humble Quest to Follow the Bible as Literally as Possible*, by A. J. Jacobs.[2] I have to admit I enjoyed reading this book. The author, who describes himself as agnostic, seemed to make an honest attempt at following every rule in the Bible for one full year. Knowing how to follow the Bible requires significant study, and Jacobs faced a steep learning curve.

This led to a number of humorous moments. For example, when the year was over, someone asked Jacobs, "Were you able to stone an adulterer?"

He replied:

> Just one. I was walking in the park dressed in full biblical attire—white clothes, sandals, a staff— and an elderly man asked me what I was doing. I explained that I was trying to abide by all the rules of the Bible, including stoning adulterers. He said, "I'm an adulterer. You gonna stone me?" And I said, "Well, yes, that would be great." I showed him some pebbles from my pocket that I had stored for just this occasion. He grabbed the pebbles out of my hand and whipped them at me. So I decided, an eye for an eye and tossed a pebble at him. And in that way I stoned.[3]

For the record, I don't think the Bible actually teaches us to stone people (see chapter 2). But I think Jacobs illustrates what most people think the Bible is all about, and his story represents the absurdity of actually following the Bible that way. What he really missed is the overarching goal of the Bible, the context in which the commands come.

Viewing the Bible as nothing more than a series of commands would be like reading a detailed book of rules that govern the game of soccer without really understanding the goal of the game. Studying tedious rules on the proper procedures for a throw-in, the exact circumstances of when an offside penalty will be assessed, and a thorough breakdown of what constitutes a foul is tiresome in any circumstance. But this is especially true if you have no concept that the way to win the game is to score more goals than the other team.

However, if you love the game of soccer and the thrill of victory, you will want to know about every rule so you have the best chance of winning. Who wants to lose possession of the ball just before kicking a winning goal because you didn't know a basic rule? At times, it seems like the Bible is like a rule book, including charts with exactly how many feet and inches all the lines on a soccer field should be (see the instructions for building the tabernacle in Exodus 26). If you focus on the rules without seeing the big picture, you won't get the point.

The Bible starts with the big picture. God is the creator of all that we see and know of in the universe. God created us, and he created us with a special purpose. Unlike everything else in creation, God made us in his "image" (Genesis 1:26). God crowned us with glory and made us rulers over all the living things he created (Psalm 8:5–6). He created us to function as creatures who will continually bring glory to him. He refers to us as a people "created for my glory" (Isaiah 43:7). We only function properly when we pursue God's glory because that is what he designed us to do.

God is not imposing a burden on us by commanding us to live for his glory. He isn't pressuring us into slave labor in his enormous project of glory seeking. He really doesn't need us in order to have glory. Rather, God structured our body and soul to glorify him because that is what he knows will bring us the most satisfaction. He designed us to want to know him and be loved by him. Therefore, we function best when we are doing what we are designed to do. When we seek other things, we become dysfunctional. We aren't equipped properly for those things.

Consider a majestic eagle. This great bird has a special design that comes with the ability to soar high through the sky. From the light but sturdy structure of his bones, to the precise way his feathers fit together, to the way his lungs can supply his body with oxygen even at high altitudes, flying is something he was made for. Now, he could do other things. He could spend his whole life sitting by a park bench, subsisting on whatever scraps were left for him by workers hanging around on their lunch break. He could travel a little bit by walking around. But if that were all he ever did, if he never stretched his wings out and plunged into the breeze and took off toward the sky, what would we think of his life? We would think, *What a waste.*

An eagle must fly to have a successful life. That's what an eagle is designed for. On the other hand, if we try to pursue success the same way, we would face utter tragedy. We are not designed to fly like an eagle. I had a friend once who tried to fly. He had it in his head that he could not be happy unless he at least gave it a shot. He longed to feel what the great birds feel, even if just for a moment. So, at the age of nine, he climbed up on the roof of his trailer and took a dramatic leap into the air. I probably don't need to tell you that it didn't go so well. Not only did he fail in his attempt to fly, but he also ended up with a broken arm.

In the same way, when we live for things we weren't designed for, sooner or later, we will crash in failure. The only path to true joy and peace is to live the way we were designed to function. If money becomes our number one goal because it seems to offer security or the ability to have the pleasures of life, it will disappoint us. No matter how much we have, we will want more. When we get more, we will be happy, but only for a time. When we lose it, we will become angry, bitter, or depressed. Even if we are very successful at obtaining money throughout life, it will not last. Eventually, everyone loses everything they have, and life is short. One way or another, money will not last long.

Living for the approval of others will also end in disappointment. When we have approval from others, we feel good—for a time. When we don't have it, we feel despair. The same is true with power, sex, and anything else people spend their lives pursuing. They are all dead ends. Not so with God. When we pursue his glory, we are living for something that cannot disappoint us. We are living the way we were designed to live by a loving God. We are living for something truly satisfying and joy-giving. God did not create us for his glory so he could boss us around, but so we could enjoy him.

The apostle Paul said it best when he wrote in a letter to a group of Christians in the city of Philippi, "Rejoice in the Lord always. I will say it again: Rejoice!" He went on in this letter to talk about "the peace of God, which transcends all understanding" and "the secret of being content in any and every situation" (Philippians 4:4, 7, 12). This was all a result of pursuing God's plan for his life, which he identified in the same letter as considering "everything a loss because of the surpassing worth of knowing Christ Jesus my Lord, for whose sake I have lost all things" (Philippians 3:8). According to Paul, the goal was hard to pursue; he had to lose "all things." This is what Jesus calls dying to self. But Paul said it was worth it. He described having a life of rest, free from burdens. Paul experienced true joy, peace, and contentment in life. That is being prosperous and successful.

Seeing this big picture of what God tells us about the goal of life helps us to understand what all the stories and commands are about. They are simply filling in the details of how to pursue this goal of life. Rather than imposing burdens, the commands are blessings. The psalmist described them this way: "How sweet are your words to my taste, sweeter than honey to my mouth" (Psalm 119:103). The stories in the Bible relate in some way to helping us understand how to live this God-glorifying life, helping us understand more about God, the problems that keep us from glorifying him, and the specific rules we need to know in order to glorify him.

## Decisions

Life is full of decisions. Every day, we make countless decisions, from what to wear to when to eat. We also make countless decisions that reflect our values and beliefs. Should I snap at my coworker or overlook his carelessness? Should I watch both football games today or go outside and play with my son? Every decision reflects what we really think is most important in life. Each one reveals our true goal.

Successful companies know that they must have a clear vision that guides everyday decisions. With a vision, a company can evaluate the pros and cons of any decision based on whether it helps them fulfill the vision. If there is no agreement on the vision, a company will struggle under the burden of constant clashes on what to do every time a decision is needed, which is every day.

Google's registration statement provides a good example of a clear vision: "Our goal is to develop services that significantly improve the lives of as many people as possible." Google also included examples in their statement about how their goal impacted their decisions. For example, they chose to support over ninety languages, not because they believed it was the easiest path to turning a profit, but because they believed it would "improve the lives of as many people as possible." They also identified selectivity in advertising, choosing to show ads that "are relevant and useful rather than intrusive and annoying." When they make a decision about advertising, they refer back to their goal of improving the lives of as many people as possible.[4]

The Bible says our goal in life is to glorify God. We may not be aware of it; we may choose to live as if we have a different goal, but that is the goal for which we were designed. Commandments in the Bible are there to help us determine which decisions support our goal and which are destructive. Sin occurs when we make decisions in life that move us away from glorifying God. For example, adultery is a sin because it is a choice that seeks to fulfill one's own desires. It is self-seeking rather than God glorifying. God has designed us to glorify him in how we treat others. Honoring marriage commitments is ultimately about honoring God with your life.

The Bible says that when we make sinful choices, life will get hard. "There will be trouble and distress for every human being who does evil" (Romans 2:9). This is the result of being self-seeking. On the other hand, the Bible promises "glory, honor and peace for everyone who does good" (Romans 2:8–10). Rather than giving a lengthy list of wearisome rules, the Bible offers us a clearly defined path to prosperity and success. Then it tells us which decisions will keep us on the path and which will lead us off the path. It does not promise that going down the path will always be easy, but it does promise that the destination is worth it. When we trust the Bible, we are not subjecting ourselves to the strict rules of an authoritarian. Instead, we trust a guide to lead us to our desired destination, even if the pathway there is full of difficulties and uncertainties.

---

1. Barna OmniPoll, "The New Moral Code," in *Good Faith,* David Kinnaman and Gabe Lyons (Grand Rapids, MI: Baker, 2016), 58.
2. A. J. Jacobs, *The Year of Living Biblically* (New York: Simon & Schuster, 2007).
3. Ibid., 392.
4. Larry Page and Sergey Brin, "2004 Founder's IPO Letter." https://abc. xyz/investor/founders-letters/2004-ipo-letter/. Accessed February 9, 2019.

# CHAPTER 2

# TRUSTING THE GUIDE

Always be prepared to give an answer to everyone who
asks you to give the reason for the hope that you have.

—1 Peter 3:15

So far, I've claimed that the proper guide to success in life is the
Bible. I've told you that the Bible identifies the goal of life: to
glorify God. I've told you that we can trust the Bible because it is
God's Word. Trusting the Bible is one and the same as trusting God.
I've also told you that we have evidence of this. God does not ask
us to blindly believe but provided Jesus as a reliable witness to the
authority and truth of the Bible.

At this point, I need to hit the pause button. Before you can
commit yourself to a life of self-denial in order to bring glory to
the deity of a small, ancient Middle Eastern nation, you may have
some questions. It is good to have some questions. If there are no
reasonable answers, it would be unadvisable to go any further.

In this chapter, I will respond to what I think are some of the
most common and important questions to ask. I will only offer a
brief answer to these questions; space will not allow me to address all
of them. I don't expect that you can or should trust the Bible simply
because of what I write in this chapter. My goal is to convince you

that there may be sufficient answers to the questions you have. If you have more doubts or questions, I encourage you to do additional research on your own. At the end of the chapter, I will recommend other books to help you dig deeper into these questions.

## How Do We Know That We Can Trust Jesus?

We can trust him if he truly rose from the dead. The resurrection provides verification that the claims Jesus made about himself are true. And if the claims Jesus made about himself are true, then we can trust him, because he is God.

Jesus's actions and statements communicated to a first-century Jewish audience that he believed he was the one true God. For example, he forgave people's sins. Now, it is normal to forgive someone when they sin against you, but it is not normal to say, "Your sins are forgiven," referring to *all* their sins. When Jesus did this, the teachers of the law made the connection, saying, "Who can forgive sins but God alone?" (Mark 2:5–7). Jesus also called himself the "bread of life" that "gives life to the world" (John 6:33–35), picturing himself as the fulfillment of a miracle God performed centuries earlier when he had bread fall from heaven to feed the Israelites (Exodus 16). Jesus even accepted worship from others. One of his disciples, Thomas, proclaimed, "My Lord and my God." Jesus offered no correction to this proclamation (John 20:28).

There are many more examples of Jesus indicating his divine status. For now, I think these are sufficient to demonstrate he was not simply a good teacher. A man who spoke and acted the way Jesus did, especially in the strict monotheistic Jewish culture of the time, had probably lost touch with reality. Alternatively, he could have been a manipulative charlatan who would say anything to get people to do what he wanted. There's also one other possibility. Perhaps he really is God. There's really no middle ground.

If Jesus rose from the dead, it shows that he was not merely crazy or deceptive. He predicted that he would be put to death and rise from the dead. He taught that the Bible had prophesied it long ago. Then, he did it.

How do we know this? You do not need to start off with the assumption that the Bible is God's Word to believe in the resurrection. Simply recognize the New Testament writings as historical documents. I'm not even saying you have to trust that everything written in them is historically accurate. However, somebody living in the past did write them, and so, at the very least, they represent a view that was expressed in the first century. Most of the New Testament books were written between fifteen and forty years after the death and resurrection of Jesus.[1] That includes at least three of the Gospels and multiple letters that also attest to the basic facts about Jesus's death, resurrection, and divine status. Many are at least partially based on even earlier sources. For example, Paul recorded an early oral tradition about the death and resurrection of Jesus in 1 Corinthians 15:3–8. Although he wrote the letter about twenty years after the resurrection, he quoted from a source that dates back to within a few years of the events.[2]

The literary style of the New Testament was not myth or fiction. The authors clearly claimed to be writing about true, historical events. They indicated familiarity with the dates, places, and customs of the time. Their descriptions can be validated by studying archaeology and other historical writings from the time. Whatever you think about Jesus, this much is clear: by the middle of the first century, there was a community of thousands in many locations who believed that Jesus was the God-man, the prophesied Messiah who was crucified, buried, and raised from the dead. Many of them continued believing and proclaiming this message in spite of severe persecution. Even skeptics of Christianity acknowledge that we know at least this much.[3]

What best accounts for their beliefs? A number of theories have been proposed, and the purpose of this book does not allow me to address each one. However, I do believe that there is only one theory that really offers a reasonable explanation of the facts: Jesus Christ really did claim to be God and really rose from the dead.

Lee Strobel was an atheist and journalist for the *Chicago Tribune* who started researching the historical evidence about Jesus in order to prove Christianity wrong. Instead, he was persuaded that the historical evidence demonstrates that Jesus really is God.[4] Another former atheist, J. Warner Wallace, is a cold-case homicide detective who used his professional investigative skills to critically evaluate the reliability of the New Testament. He reports, "Within a month, and in spite of my deep skepticism and hesitation, I concluded that Mark's Gospel was the eyewitness account of the apostle Peter. I was beginning to move from a belief *that* Jesus was a wise teacher to a belief *in* what he said about himself."[5] If you have questions about who Jesus really is, I encourage you to do your own research and come to your own conclusions.

## How Do We Even Know That God Exists?

One of the main objections to the resurrection, and thus the divinity of Jesus, is that miracles don't happen. God doesn't exist, or even if he does, we have no reason to think he interferes with the normal course of events in our world. Consider Bart Ehrman, one of the world's greatest scholars on the New Testament and a self-described agnostic.[6] He agrees that the New Testament documents and other historical sources are early records about the life of Jesus. He agrees that Jesus's followers believed that he was crucified and rose from the dead from the very first year or couple of years after his earthly ministry. However, Ehrman rejects that the resurrection is the best explanation for the single reason that a resurrection would be a miracle, and miracles don't happen. He writes that any other explanation of the resurrection occurring is more likely, "no matter how unlikely" it may be.[7]

What you believe about God's existence and the possibility of his involvement with the earth will determine how you evaluate the rest of the evidence for the Bible. If you conclude that things like resurrections can't happen, then you won't believe Jesus rose from the dead, no matter how much evidence you have. Ehrman even acknowledges that every nonmiraculous explanation for the resurrection is highly unlikely from a historian's perspective. He doesn't reject Jesus's resurrection because of the evidence; he rejects it because he won't even consider it as a possibility from the outset.

However, what if Ehrman's view about miracles is incorrect? If God is real, then miracles are possible. I would go further and say miracles would be expected. It seems odd to imagine a god creating a world with beings like us and never again having any involvement with his creation. No, if God is real, we should expect to find evidence of him at work in our world in the form of miracles. If miracles are real, then the only significant historical objection to the truth of the resurrection is gone. The resurrection, and subsequently the truth of the Bible, would be the only reasonable conclusion.

So does God exist? Let me start with an easier question: "Is it unreasonable to believe that everything in the universe has come about with no god at all?" I think it is unreasonable to believe such a thing, and the only alternative is some kind of god. At this point, I'm not trying to prove that there is a god. I'm simply saying it is much more reasonable to believe there is one. If you agree with at least that much, then it is reasonable to believe that the God who created us would have some purpose for us and would want to communicate that purpose to us. From there, we could look at the world's religions and see if there is a match, if there is evidence that God really has spoken to us through a particular person or book.

Why do I say it is unreasonable to believe that the universe has come about with no god at all? There are simply too many things that are difficult to explain if there is no god. I am appealing to a sense of what is reasonable and unreasonable, a standard we all use to shape our view of reality all the time. Most of our beliefs are based on choosing between different explanations for why things are the way they are. We prefer explanations that don't leave unanswered questions, create additional questions, or require unlikely scenarios.

For example, we believe that the Earth is round because there are simply too many things that are hard to explain if it isn't. You probably haven't actually seen the roundness of the Earth by orbiting it from the International Space Station, but you trust that the images of a round Earth on television, the testimony of astronauts, and countless scientific articles and textbooks are correct. To believe otherwise would require you to come up with an explanation for all sorts of contrary data, leaving many unanswered questions in your mind.

I have encountered people on social media who believe that the Earth is flat. I cannot agree with them because they just don't have adequate answers to the many questions raised by their position. They allege that the roundness of the Earth is all part of a huge conspiracy, that photos from space are all forgeries, and that scientists have lied to us about things like the cause of tides and the distances to the moon and sun. I cannot prove them wrong, nor would I bother to go to much effort to try. Their theory simply doesn't hold up in my mind because they have no good answers to so many other questions. Who started this lie? What was their motive? Why are so many people involved in perpetuating this lie? No, I think the view that the Earth is round is much more satisfactory.

In the same way, the idea that there is no god simply provokes too many challenging questions. For instance, why do the physical laws of the universe seem to be set in exactly the right way for the universe to allow for the possibility of life? Physicist Paul Davies notes that if neutrons, one of the subatomic particles, were lighter by a fraction of 1 percent, then atoms and molecules could not exist. He adds that any changes in the strengths of the four forces of nature would make life impossible in the universe.[8]

Stephen Hawking also observes, "The laws of science, as we know them at present, contain many fundamental numbers, like the size of the electric charge of the electron and the ratio of the masses of the proton and the electron; the remarkable fact is that the values of these numbers seem to have been very finely adjusted to make possible the development of life."[9] The precision with which the various variables in the universe match those required for life is strong evidence that the universe was purposefully designed with life in mind.

How can you make sense of the universe's fine-tuning without God? Furthermore, how could nonliving matter and purposeless physical processes alone lead to the formation of the complex machines that make up life? Where did the first living beings come from? In addition, how could these amazing little creatures then develop into beings who can intelligently debate the existence of a divine creator? The questions go on and on.

If there is no creator, there is no reason to believe that our thinking processes are capable of leading us to truth. Our brains would have developed solely under evolutionary processes that promote survival, not the ability to discern the truth about the nature of the universe. The very concept of a rational debate about God's existence strongly suggests God's existence. C. S. Lewis, an atheist professor turned Christian, explained, "In the very act of trying to prove that God did not exist—in other words, that the whole of reality was senseless—I found I was forced to assume that one part of reality—namely my idea of justice—was full of sense. Consequently atheism turns out to be too simple. If the whole universe has no meaning, we should never have found out that it has no meaning."[10]

And what about suffering? Yes, atheists usually bring up suffering to charge that there can be no all-powerful God, at least not a good one. Yet, if there is no God, how could there be suffering? Suffering would just be an illusion, a perception of pain that our faculties have created to help us survive and pass on in our genes. We perceive real suffering when we sense that the universe is not the way it should be. But with no God, there is no way the universe should be; it just is. My experiences with suffering prevent me from accepting that it is just an illusion. I believe suffering is real. I believe that God is real.

Not only do I believe that God is real, but it makes little sense to me that this God would make creatures like us unless he wanted us to know him. Not just know of him, or about him, but know him. Why else would he create us with the ability to study nature in a way that points us to him, to have experiences that point us to him, to have rational faculties that enable us to debate his existence, unless he wanted us to "seek him and perhaps reach out for him and find him" (Acts 17:27)?

Now, could I be wrong about all this? Sure, at this point, I haven't proven that God exists. But I do think that at the very least, I have given sufficient reason to go out and look for him. Given the information we have and the experiences we share in life, it is only reasonable to expect that God is real and that he would want to communicate with us. If we are unable to find a match, we could at best say it is probable that there is a god, but we would have no way of knowing one way or the other for sure because we have no way of knowing anything about him. We would be forced into agnosticism.

But do we have a match? Is there evidence that a personal God who wants to contact us has actually appeared in history? I believe I have found this match in the God revealed in the Bible and especially in Jesus. I do not think it is a mere coincidence that Jesus fits precisely with what we should already expect to find in the universe: a God who created and designed us and cares greatly about us. Jesus is the best reason for believing that God exists.

## Is There Only One True Religion?

It's hard to say that there is only one right religion and all others are wrong. It sounds arrogant. Something about it makes us feel uncomfortable. However, the truth is what matters most, even if it doesn't always feel good. For instance, it may not be easy for a doctor to tell a patient that she will die without a difficult surgery, but it would be wrong for the doctor to keep that information a secret in order to avoid a difficult conversation.

The truth is that it is impossible for all religions to be right. According to Islam, I will go to hell when I die. I have committed blasphemy by worshiping Jesus as God while failing to recognize Mohammad as God's greatest prophet. According to Christianity, I will go to heaven because Jesus forgave all my sins when I trusted in him as my Lord and Savior. Hindu religions say I will be born again on this earth through reincarnation. Atheists say that my body will decay and there is nothing more to it. Only one of these can be right. I cannot simultaneously go to heaven and hell when I die. There is only one of me, and I have to go somewhere! As uncomfortable as it may make us feel, the inescapable conclusion is that the majority of people are wrong about the afterlife.

But is it possible to know which religion is true? Must everyone simply make the best guess with the information they have and hope they guess correctly? A quick scan of the world's religions would make it appear so. However, Christianity stands out among other religions because it presents the opportunity for objective evaluation. The kind of evidence that supports the Christian faith is different from the kind of evidence that supports other religions.

For example, consider the evidence for Islam. The authoritative teachings for Muslims are found in the Koran. Muhammad claimed that an angel gave him the words that were eventually recorded in the Koran. That's a remarkable claim, but is it true? How can we know? Basically, we have to believe what Muhammad said. How do we know that this angel appeared to Muhammad? Muhammad said so. How do we know that the words he taught were the words that came from the angel? Muhammad said so. Even assuming that a supernatural being did appear to him, how do we know that it was a good angel and not a bad one? The answer is always, "Muhammad said so." Whether Islam is true or not comes down to whether we can trust Muhammad.

Not so with Christianity. The Christian faith is not based on a private event that was only witnessed by one person. Instead, it is based on the public death and resurrection of Jesus. These were historical events seen by hundreds of people. There is documented evidence of these events from numerous sources. You can study the evidence. You may be persuaded by the historical evidence or you may deny it, but at least you can evaluate evidence rather than simply going on, "So-and-so said so."

All religions I have studied besides Christianity run into a similar problem. Mormonism claims that Joseph Smith received help from an angel translating special golden tablets. How do we know this? Joseph Smith tells us so. There is no other way to corroborate the claims. There are statements from a few who attest to having seen the golden plates, but no one other than Joseph Smith ever claimed to know what was written on them or how to translate them. You simply have to believe because Joseph Smith says so.

Other religious texts, such as the Vedas of Hinduism, do not even have a known author or origin. They do not claim that a historical person received divine revelation at a specific time and place. Therefore, the truth of their teaching does not depend on trusting a particular person. But this makes matters even worse. The only way to evaluate their credibility is to examine the teachings themselves and decide for yourself whether you believe they are true. I don't know about you, but I simply don't trust myself that much. I don't believe that in my limited time on this earth, I can read the religious books from various places around the world and say, "That's it; that one has it right more than all the others." How could anyone have such knowledge?

Christianity offers a way out of the uncertainty. It offers an objective way to analyze evidence. I may not be smart enough to figure out which set of religious teachings are true from a philosophical standpoint, but I can follow historical evidence to find out what is true. I don't trust my own judgment on spiritual truth, but I can trust someone who claimed to be God, who told us he came to die on a cross and to rise from the dead, and who did just that. I can look at historical evidence supporting public events in order to verify Christianity.

## Why Does the Bible Contain Silly Stories That Belong to Primitive People?

The Bible was written with a very wide audience in mind: every human being on the planet! It was written to everyone from simple hunter-gatherers in the Amazon rainforests to the CEOs of the leading companies advancing computer technology. It reflects a great deal of cultural bias to say that the Bible cannot be God's Word because it doesn't fit with the expected writing style of a well-educated twenty-first-century American.

Jesus once said that God "causes his sun to rise on the evil and the good" (Matthew 5:45). We can scoff at that and say, "Doesn't

Jesus know that the sun doesn't actually 'rise,' but only appears to do so because of the earth's rotation?" Yet we employ the same figure of speech in our language when we talk about "sunrises" and "sunsets." The Bible was not written like a college physics book, a history student's PhD dissertation on ancient Egypt, or a peer-reviewed article in a journal on human psychology. If it were, it would have been almost completely inaccessible to most of the world's population right up to the present time.

The Bible is often criticized as low-level writing compared to us moderns. Clearly, critics will say, the differences between Genesis 1 and 2 show that a sloppy editor patched together two incompatible creation accounts. They fail to account for the intricate structures of ancient literature that are common among oral cultures. The Bible frequently uses chiastic structures to heighten comparison and contrasts between various events (see an example in the chart below).

## Chiastic Structure of Genesis 12:1–21:7[11]

A. Introduction: Abram's journey to Canaan and the promise of descendants (12:1–9).

  B. Abram lies about Sarai in Egypt; God protects her in foreign king's court (12:10–20).

    C. Lot settles in Sodom (13:1–18).

      D. Abram intercedes for Lot and Sodom militarily (14:1–24).

        E. Promise of a son for Abraham (15:1–21).

          F. Ishmael's birth (16:1–16).

            Center. Yahweh's covenant; Abram and Sarai's names changed (17:1–21).

          F'. Ishmael and Abraham circumcised (17:22–27).

        E'. Promise of a son from Sarai herself (18:1–15).

      D'. Abraham intercedes for Sodom and Lot in prayer (18:16–33).

    C'. Lot flees Sodom (19:1–38).

  B'. Abraham lies about Sarah in Gerar; God protects her in foreign king's court (20:1–18).

A'. Conclusion: birth of Isaac (fulfillment of promise begins) (21:1–7).

When I first discovered chiastic structures in the Bible, I felt like I was reading many familiar passages for the first time. New layers of meaning and understanding opened up. Biblical stories are powerful and have fueled the imagination of people on multiple continents for thousands of years. There are reasons for this, even if the biblical literary structure isn't immediately evident to the modern reader.

As for that silly story about a talking snake, it may not be that silly. If you assume the Bible is a childish book, you may be quick to believe that its stories are childish. But for those who dig a little deeper, believing the text to be communication from the divine and infinitely wise creator, surprises abound. For instance, the Hebrew word for "snake" used in Genesis 3 is *nachash*. It is the same root word that also means "diviner." Practicing divination in the Bible always refers to communication with the supernatural world. There is a reason why ancient traditions understood that Eve was encountering a powerful supernatural being represented by a snake.[12] The text subtly tells us so by using a word with a double meaning. Reading the Bible is not reverting back to childhood; rather, it is full of mysteries to unravel and adventures to enjoy.

## Haven't People Changed What the Bible Says Many Times?

In the telephone game, a message is passed from one person to another by whispering into each individual's ear. With every transfer, the message changes slightly. After a while, the original message is unrecognizable. Could something like this have happened with the Bible?

We know that it did not because the Bible has a long paper trail to verify that it was not changed. Ancient manuscripts are regularly lost because of fires, shipwrecks, or just plain wearing out from age. Nevertheless, the messages of many of these texts are known to us because people hand-copied them over and over again. Most ancient books have few copies (if any) still in existence that were made within a thousand years of the original writing. However, the New Testament has at least 838 manuscripts that date within a thousand years of the originals. This is far more than any other source from a similar time period. The New Testament also has many more early copies of texts compared to other works. In fact, there are three times as many New Testament manuscripts dating within two hundred years of the original writings as there are for the average classical author's work within two thousand years of composition.[13]

This bulky paper trail of manuscripts gives Bible scholars the ability to compare texts from different time periods to see if any changes were made. For example, some people allege that Constantine changed the Bible in the fourth century, perhaps because they have seen the movie *The DaVinci Code*, a fictional story. However, scholars can examine seventy-six manuscripts made in the second and third centuries (before Constantine). When they compare them with later manuscripts, they find no evidence that someone tampered with the text.[14]

Others allege that the problem is not with the manuscripts themselves but with the translation process. If the Bible were translated from Greek and Hebrew to Latin, then from Latin to French, and so on, then the telephone game would be a reasonable comparison. But that is not how translations work. Instead, modern English translations go back to the original Greek and Hebrew texts of the Bible, as assembled by textual scholars who carefully compare the thousands of ancient manuscripts to determine what the original text said. There are many English versions of the Bible today, but not because the Bible keeps changing. Rather, it is because the English language keeps changing. People do not talk the same way in twenty-first-century America as they did in England in 1611 when the King James Version was translated.

New translations also result from different goals in the translation process. Some translators try to stay very close to the words and word order of the Greek text, while others focus on capturing the meaning of a Greek phrase or sentence in more natural-sounding English. However, there is no evidence that Bibles are getting further away from the original text today than they were near the time of the originals.

The story of how we got from the original writings of the

Bible to the modern English Bibles of today is rather remarkable. According to the evidence, we have greater reason to trust that we know the original text of the Bible better than any other ancient literature. The extraordinary preservation of the text of the Bible makes sense if God has worked through history to safeguard his word, but it would be astonishing if it is all just coincidence.

## What about All the Contradictions in the Bible?

Matthew tells us that Judas died when "he went away and hanged himself" (Matthew 27:5). In the book of Acts, Luke does not say Judas hanged himself. Instead, he reports that Judas "fell headlong, his body burst open and all his intestines spilled out" (Acts 1:8). Bible critics point to hundreds of examples like this in order to say the accounts are not trustworthy. "With such wildly different versions of basic events," they ask, "who knows what really happened?"

In reality, this example and many others like it are not true contradictions. It would be a contradiction if Matthew said that Judas hanged himself and Luke said that Judas *did not* hang himself, but Luke says no such thing. Matthew and Luke could easily be describing the same event. Matthew tells us the bare facts: Judas hanged himself. Luke gives us a more complete and graphic depiction of Judas' grisly demise. Once Judas hanged himself, his body began to toughen as it began to decompose in the sun. Eventually, the rope was cut down, and his body fell on the rocks below. He "fell headlong," and he "burst open." You may wince picturing this in your mind; that is what Luke intended.

We do not know for sure that Luke is telling us what happened after Judas hanged himself, but we have no reason to believe that he is contradicting Matthew's account. Different authors write with different perspectives and purposes. Matthew was a former friend of Judas and wanted to move quickly to the next topic. Luke did not know Judas personally and wanted to emphasize what happened to a traitor. The Bible is full of these kinds of discrepancies, but I do not know of any genuine contradictions.

Differences in accounts like the ones about Judas actually add credibility to the historical reliability of their claims. When police are documenting eyewitness testimony about an accident, they do not want one person's testimony to influence another's. Multiple witnesses may start their statements in a different place, leave out or include specific details, or have different emotional reactions depending on if they were involved in the accident or were just nearby. However, if the testimonies agree on the basic facts, a core story emerges that the police can have confidence in. If, however, multiple witnesses say the exact same things, the police may be suspicious that they talked together to get their story straight ahead of time. In the same way, the differences in the Bible tell us that we have independent, eyewitness testimonies about the life, death, and resurrection of Jesus.

## Am I Really Supposed to Follow All the Commands in the Bible?

Often people hear about commands like not eating shellfish or stoning adulterers and conclude that following the Bible is totally absurd. However, the Bible itself does not say everyone should follow all the commands. Instead, each person should follow all that the Bible commands *them* to do.

For example, in Genesis 12:1, the Bible records God's command to "go from your country, your people and your father's household to the land I will show you." Now, if you are supposed to follow all that the Bible commands, then you must immediately head toward the nearest international airport and leave the country. However, the verse is not commanding you to do this. Only one person living in a particular place was commanded to do this. In context, the verse says, "The LORD had said to Abram [Abraham], 'Go from your country.'" Nothing in the text suggests that everyone needs to leave their country; only Abraham was told to leave the land he was in.

Now, the command to "go from your country" is still God's Word. You can learn from it, and God can speak to you through it. For instance, you may learn that following God at times requires a willingness to make major changes in life. Perhaps you believe that

God is leading you to change jobs so you can spend more time with your family. Seeing Abraham step out in faith to obey a difficult command from God could encourage you to do the right thing in your job situation. However, you do not have to move to Israel, as Abraham did, in order to be obedient to God.

The same thing is true with all the commands in the Bible. You can profit from all of them without necessarily obeying them directly. You must carefully discern which commands address you, such as "love your neighbor," and which commands are instructive but not necessarily for you to obey personally. The Bible itself tells us when a command is for all people and when a command is for a specific nation, person, or circumstance.

For instance, the Bible describes a number of commands related to keeping the "Sabbath day" holy. These include, "Do not light a fire in any of your dwellings on the Sabbath day" (Exodus 35:3). But the context tells us that these commands were only for the nation of Israel. "Say to the Israelites, 'You must observe my Sabbaths. This will be a sign between me and you for the generations to come'" (Exodus 31:13). People from other nations can learn from these commands and observe a kind of Sabbath today based on the principle of Sabbath keeping that God gave the Israelites. In some sense, the Sabbath is for everyone, because Jesus said, "The Sabbath was made for man, not man for the Sabbath" (Mark 2:27). However, only the Israelites were required to follow a specific list of regulations on the Sabbath day. The New Testament never tells Christians from other nations that they must observe all the Sabbath regulations given to Israelites.

The same thing is true about shellfish. The command forbidding shellfish is found in Leviticus 11, which addresses the Israelites. If you are not Jewish, this is not a command directed toward you. God gave many commands to Israel that he never gave to other nations. Why? The reason is that Israel has always had a special role to play in God's plan. God used Israel to write the Bible, prepare the way for Jesus the Messiah, and begin the work of preaching about Jesus to the nations. Dietary laws were a special way that God set Israel apart and prepared them for their unique role. Generally, animals that eat living things were allowed, while animals that eat waste or dead animals were forbidden.

The Israelites were to eat this way to pay special attention to how they prepared themselves to worship and be a part of God's special nation. It's not that there is anything inherently sinful about the act of eating shellfish. Similarly, there is nothing necessarily sinful about wearing jeans and a T-shirt. However, it would be offensive to wear an outfit like that in the Oval Office while meeting with the president. In the same way, God was giving a special dress code just for the Israelites as they fulfilled his special role for them. Today, Christians from other nations can study these commands and learn to pursue God in every area of life. However, everyone is not required to refrain from eating shrimp in order to be part of the Christian community.

Now consider the command to stone an adulterer that caused a dilemma for A. J. Jacobs, the man who "tossed a pebble" at an adulterer in order to live biblically back in chapter 1. The key passage is Deuteronomy 22:22, which actually doesn't mention stoning but does say that adulterers should be put to death. Tossing a pebble at someone does not count as following the command literally because the verse says to put them to death, not annoy them with a pebble.

More importantly, throwing stones is actually not following the command at all. That is because the context shows that this verse was given to Israelites living in the nation of Israel who were living under the covenant with Moses and acting as a governing community. The context required an Israelite judge and a trial with witnesses. An individual was never commanded to stone an adulterer. A gentile was never commanded to stone an adulterer. A Jew living in a foreign country was never commanded to stone an adulterer. Today, even if you are a Jew, even if you are in Israel, even if you are acting as part of a governing community, you are not required to stone an adulterer because the government of Israel isn't set up to reestablish Mosaic law as the rule for the nation, as the context of the passage requires.

Instead, a Christian is commanded to "submit himself to the governing authorities" (Romans 13:1). If I throw a rock at an adulterer, I am committing assault and am directly violating the biblical command to follow the law of the land. That is living *un*biblically. Christians are often accused of picking and choosing which commands they follow and which ones they ignore. In some cases, that may be true; I can't speak for every Christian. However, Christians who follow the Bible according to the Joshua 1:8 promise and seek to do everything written in it should never pick and choose. Rather, they must allow the Bible itself to control how the commands are followed by paying attention to context.

## For Further Reading

Copan, Paul. *When God Goes to Starbucks*. Grand Rapids, MI: Baker, 2008.

Cowan, Steven B., ed. *In Defense of the Bible*. Nashville: Broadman & Holman, 2013.

Geisler, Norman, and Thomas Howe. *The Big Book of Bible Difficulties*. Grand Rapids, MI: Baker, 2008.

Geisler, Norman, and Frank Turek. *I Don't Have Enough Faith to be an Atheist*, Wheaton, IL: Crossway Books, 2004.

Strobel, Lee. *The Case for Christ,* Grand Rapids, MI: Zondervan, 1998.

Wallace, J. Warner. *Cold-Case Christianity: A Homicide Detective Discusses the Claims of Christianity.* Colorado Springs: David C. Cook, 2013.

---

1. Norman Geisler and Frank Turek, *I Don't Have Enough Faith to Be an Atheist* (Wheaton, IL: Crossway Books, 2004), 243–44.
2. Paul W. Barnett, "Is the New Testament Historically Reliable?" in *In Defense of the Bible*, eds. Steven B. Cowan and Terry L. Wilder (Nashville: Broadman & Holman, 2013).
3. See, for example, Bart D. Ehrman, *How Jesus Became God* (New York: Harper One, 2014), 138, 174.
4. Lee Strobel, *The Case for Christ* (Grand Rapids, MI: Zondervan, 2016).
5. J. Warner Wallace, *Cold-Case Christianity* (Colorado Springs: David C. Cook, 2013), 19.
6. Ehrman, *How Jesus Became God,* 354.
7. Bart D. Ehrman, *Did Jesus Exist?* (New York: Harper One, 2012), 173.

8. Paul Davies, *The Cosmic Jackpot* (New York: Houghton Mifflin, 2007), 145, 150.

9. Stephen Hawking, *The Illustrated A Brief History of Time* (New York: Bantam, 1996), 160.

10. C. S. Lewis, *Mere Christianity* (Nashville: Broadman & Holman, 1996), 46.

11. David A. Dorsey, *The Literary Structure of the Old Testament* (Grand Rapids, MI: Baker Academic, 1999), 56.

12. Michael Heiser, *The Unseen Realm* (Bellingham, WA: Lexham, 2015), 87–88.

13. Daniel B. Wallace, "Has the New Testament Text Been Hopelessly Corrupted?" In *In Defense of the Bible*, eds. Steven B. Cowan and Terry L. Wilder (Nashville: Broadman & Holman, 2013), 147.

14. Ibid., 147–48.

---

## ∼⊙ CHAPTER 3 ⊙∼

# GETTING STARTED PURSUING SUCCESS

---

I am the vine; you are the branches. If you remain in me and I in you, you will bear much fruit; apart from me you can do nothing.

—John 15:5

So far, I've established that the Bible claims that being prosperous and successful in life depends upon meditating on and carefully obeying its teachings. I've given you some reasons to consider trusting that this claim is true. I've also explained that if you do choose to follow the Bible's path to success, you need to know where you are heading. You need to identify the proper goal of life. The Bible says that your goal should be to bring glory to God, no matter what personal sacrifice is required. When you do this, you can expect peace, joy, and fulfillment in life.

Now it's time to get into the nuts and bolts. How do you do this? Specifically, this chapter will address how to get started. It's not enough to know your destination and identify the vehicle that will take you there. You need to get gas, have the key, turn the car on, put it in drive, and get going down the road.

Paul's letter to the Romans identifies one of the ways to do this: "To those who by persistence in doing good seek glory, honor and immortality, he will give eternal life" (Romans 2:7). The key is to do good with "persistence." "Seeking glory" means God's glory, for this is contrasted with those who are "self-seeking" in Romans 2:8. So, if you persistently do good and seek God's glory as the most important thing in your life, the Bible promises that God will give you eternal life.

But there's a big problem with pursuing prosperity and success this way. There is bad news that the Bible tells us we need to know before we go on any further. After describing what we must do to succeed in Romans 2:7, Paul continued by saying that no one has ever actually done this: "There is no one righteous, not even one; there is no one who understands; there is no one who seeks God. All have turned away, they have together become worthless; there is no one who does good, not even one ... for all have sinned and fall short of the glory of God" (Romans 3:10–12, 23).

In Romans 3:23, "glory" has an unusual meaning. It refers to approval. Another example of when *glory* is used this way is in John 12:43: "for they loved the glory that comes from man more than the glory that comes from God" (ESV).[1] In this instance, the people who loved the glory that comes from man were hesitating to publicly profess belief in Jesus for fear of being expelled from the synagogue. They loved having man's glory, meaning approval. Falling "short of the glory of God" means failing to meet God's standards of righteousness; it means failing to obtain his approval as one who is persistent in doing good.

The Bible says that all of us fail to win God's approval because we do not live for his glory, as he created us to do. We reject God every time we choose to do things our way rather than his way. The Bible emphasizes this bad news by telling us that we are natural enemies of God: "Once you were alienated from God and were enemies in your minds because of your evil behavior" (Colossians 1:21). We are enemies because we act against God and because God's just condemnation hangs over us. The Bible calls this God's wrath. "All of us also lived among them at one time, gratifying the cravings of our flesh and following its desires and thoughts. Like the rest, we were by nature deserving of wrath" (Ephesians 2:3).

So what can we do? I still vividly remember one of my childhood transgressions. As a nine-year-old boy, I was interested in making models. I had a kit for constructing a boat and carefully glued together all the small plastic pieces. The time came for me to add color to my project with the modeling paint. I was working in my bedroom, and my grandmother instructed me to put newspaper down on the floor in the area I was working. I needed to make sure that if a drop of paint fell to the floor, it would fall on the newspaper and not the carpet.

Of course, I thought I knew better. Why bother taking the time to get newspaper out? I wanted to get started painting right away. Brimming with confidence that my cautious painting technique would render newspapers unnecessary, I began the task. I think I made it all of about three minutes before it happened. A tiny drop of red paint fell from the brush. I watched it, as if it were falling in slow motion, helpless to do anything to stop it. And there it was: a quarter-inch red glob of paint on the light, tan carpet in the middle of my bedroom.

The strong feeling of guilt swept over me immediately. What was I going to do? I started working on this problem in my mind. How could I get rid of this stain? How could I make it as if I had not disobeyed? I had no excuse for failing to heed my instructions. My only recourse was to make the stain go away. That is when I had a great idea. Since I was supposed to have newspaper down on the floor, why not put it down now, over the paint-stained spot on the carpet? That way, it will appear that I was following instructions, and there would be no way for my grandmother to see my disobedience.

Once I laid the newspaper down, I was excited about the brilliance of my plan. However, I quickly fell to despair, realizing that this would only buy me a little time. Eventually, I knew I was going to have to pick the newspaper up, and my sin would find me out. All I could do was drag out this modeling project as long as possible. Perhaps I could get started on another one as soon as I finished. After a week of thinking this way, I began to do the math in my head. "Since I'm nine now, I will need to keep this up for nine more years. Then I'll be eighteen and can move out, never having been discovered." But could I keep this up that long? "No," I decided. So I needed a new plan. Perhaps I could remove the stain myself.

I ran to the bathroom and looked under the sink, where I knew I could find a variety of cleaning products. I didn't know which one would be best, but I figured if I grabbed all of them, one of them was bound to work. With my grandmother occupied at the other end of the house, I commenced with my work. I sprayed and scrubbed with one cleaner after another. Initially, I made no progress. In fact, it seemed as if the spot was growing. Perhaps I was merely smearing the paint over a bigger area. I scrubbed harder and sprayed more cleaner, but the spot was still growing. Suddenly to my horror, I realized what was happening. One of the cleaners must have had bleach in it. That little tiny spot of paint was turning into a nearly foot-wide circle of bright orange, with no possible way to wash it out. My only option now (after a few more days of delay while a cloud of guilt hung over me) was to tell the truth and face the consequences.

The Bible says that we will fail in all our attempts to overcome sin in our lives. Nothing we do will make the stains go away. We can try to do good deeds to compensate for the bad. However, the good we do doesn't make up for the bad because all of our good deeds are things we were *supposed* to do anyway. Jesus said, "So you also, when you have done everything you were told to do, should say, 'We are unworthy servants; we have only done our duty'" (Luke 17:10).

We might also try harder to stop breaking God's commands. But there are two problems with this approach. First, we will continue to break God's law, even if we improve some. Second, this will do nothing to remove the guilt we already have because of our disobedience: "By the works of the law no one will be justified" (Galatians 2:16). Certainly, hiding our sin from God will not work either: "Nothing in all creation is hidden from God's sight. Everything is uncovered and laid bare before the eyes of him to whom we must give account" (Hebrews 4:13).

It may seem that we have hit a dead end on the journey of being prosperous and successful. However, Paul does not end with the bad news in Romans 3:23: "For all have sinned and fall short of the glory of God." He continues with the good news: "And all are justified freely by his grace through the redemption that came by Christ Jesus" (Romans 3:23–24).

Sometimes, when we are accused of doing something wrong, we try to justify ourselves. This means that we explain why what we did was not wrong. For example, if a teacher asked, "Why were you late this morning?" You could justify yourself with a doctor's note that shows where you were and what you were doing. You had an excuse for your tardiness. Having justified yourself, you are no longer guilty in the teacher's eyes.

When it comes to our sin, we have no way to justify ourselves. We really are guilty. However, God offers to justify every sin we've ever committed as a free gift to us. He offers to take the stain of our sin away. "Though your sins are like scarlet, they shall be as white as snow" (Isaiah 1:18). God offers to give this justification "through faith in Jesus Christ to all who believe" (Romans 3:22).

This gift, what the Bible calls being saved, has a whole series of wonderful implications. Salvation is not merely the way to get into heaven, as if it only addresses where we will be located after we die. According to the Bible, entrance into heaven is a result of being saved but not the thing itself.

## Salvation

Salvation is primarily the restoration of our relationship with God. Jesus explained that salvation is crossing over "from death to life," which he equated with not being "judged" (John 5:24). Later, he defined eternal life: "that they may know you, the only true God" (John 17:3). "Knowing" does not refer to knowledge about God but our relationship with him. Sin broke our relationship with God; having our sin forgiven opens the way to restoring that relationship. The Bible also describes this as being adopted into his family: "Yet to all who did receive him, to those who believed in his name, he gave the right to become children of God" (John 1:12).

Imagine you broke the law. You committed armed robbery, and now the police are looking for you. Since you don't want to get caught, you get nervous going out in public. You hide anytime you see a police officer around. Your ability to participate in public life is virtually eliminated. The mere sight of the police causes a surge of fear that you may be caught.

Now suppose you are captured, brought to trial, and sentenced. After serving the full ten years of your sentence in prison, you are released. Now you are free to go out in public again. You have nothing to fear from the police because you have already paid for your crime. You don't have to go into hiding every time you think a police officer might be somewhere. Even if the police officer knows who you are and what you did, you have no reason for concern. You cannot be convicted for the same crime again. You are now free.

This is something like what happens when you receive God's gift of eternal life. The punishment for your sin is paid for, although in this case, someone else paid it for you. Now, when God sees you, he no longer perceives a need to judge. The punishment was already carried out when Jesus went to the cross. "Therefore, there is now no condemnation for those who are in Christ Jesus" (Romans 8:1).

This is a great change in our status. Before, God had wrath toward us; now, all wrath is removed. Christians often say something like, "I believe I'll go to heaven when I die, but I sure will have a lot of explaining to do." That is a fundamental misunderstanding of the good news of the Bible. It is not about getting to heaven despite the fact that God is not happy with you. It's about God being happy about you. It's actually about not having a lot of explaining to do. There's nothing for you to explain. That's what it means to be justified. You are free from all condemnation. Going to heaven is just one of the additional results.

The Bible also says that salvation changes more than our status. God changes our direction in life. In some mysterious way, we are "crucified with Christ" (Galatians 2:20). The old person we once were was under the power of sin. Now that person is put to death. In addition, just as Jesus was raised from the dead, we also are given a new life. "If we have been united with him in a death like his, we will certainly also be united with him in a resurrection like his" (Romans 6:5).

Consequently, we are now free from the power of sin. Our union with Jesus in his death and resurrection makes it possible for us to follow God's plan to live for his glory. "But thanks be to God that, though you used to be slaves to sin, you have come to obey from your heart the pattern of teaching that has now claimed your allegiance" (Romans 6:17). The Bible gives many other wonderful descriptions of this new life in Christ. Jesus called it being "born again" (John 3:3). Paul wrote that "God raised us up with Christ and seated us with him in the heavenly realms in Christ Jesus, in order that in the coming ages he might show the incomparable riches of his grace" (Ephesians 2:6–7). Our relationship with God is now so close that he sends "the Spirit of his Son into our hearts" (Galatians 4:6). And yes, because we have a right relationship with God, we will be welcomed into heaven when we die, and we will live with God forever.

## Receiving Salvation

All these gifts are received through faith in Jesus. It is not enough to know about salvation. You must personally trust in Jesus to save you. Paul proclaimed, "We, too, have put our faith in Christ Jesus that we may be justified by faith in Christ" (Galatians 2:16). Putting your faith in Jesus is not the same thing as repeating a prayer, responding to an invitation at the end of a church service, or getting baptized. Those things may happen at the same time that you put your faith in Jesus, but they are merely outward acts that may or may not indicate saving faith.

What does it mean to put your faith in Jesus? The Bible describes a faith response in a number of different ways. Paul said, "Believe in the Lord Jesus, and you will be saved" (Acts 16:31). "Believe" is the verb that corresponds to the noun "faith" in Greek. However, the Bible also uses the word "repent" to describe what someone must do to be saved. Peter preached, "Repent, then, and turn to God, so that your sins may be wiped out" (Acts 3:19). On another occasion, Paul used both "repentance" and "faith" together: "I have declared to both Jews and Greeks that they must turn to God in repentance and have faith in our Lord Jesus" (Acts 20:21).

I should also mention Romans 10:9, which seems to add another variation: "If you declare with your mouth, 'Jesus is Lord,' and believe in your heart that God raised him from the dead, you will be saved." It may sound as if there is disagreement in the Bible about what we must do to be saved. Which is it: "repent," "believe," "repent and believe," or "declare 'Jesus is Lord' and believe in the resurrection"?

I do not believe these options are contradictions. Rather, each phrase emphasizes a different aspect of the same kind of response. You must believe in the Lord Jesus. You are trusting that what he did makes payment for your sin. You also trust him as the Lord of your life. That is repentance. You cannot believe in Jesus the Savior but reject Jesus the Lord. You believe in all of him or none of him. We are saved when we believe in him.

Suppose I was making plans to visit your hometown. I spoke with you on the phone a week ahead of time and told you where I was going. "Can you tell me which restaurants are really good?" I ask. "I believe in you," I add, letting you know that I am counting on your recommendation. "There's an amazing Italian place downtown at the intersection of Third Street and Seventh Avenue," you reply. Once I get to your town, I pass by the restaurant while I'm on my way to dinner. I decide to go somewhere else. *I just don't think it looks that good,* I think to myself. My actions demonstrate that I don't really believe in you. My expression of confidence in you was insincere. I cannot believe in you and dismiss that what you say is best for me.

Repentance is really about embracing God's plan for you to be prosperous and successful. Repentance says, "I've tried to do it my way; now I'm going to do it God's way." Why? Because I believe in Jesus. I receive his forgiveness because I know I can't pay for my own sins. Furthermore, I trust that everything he commands is really what's best for me. If he loved me enough to die for me, I must trust that he loves me in what he commands as well. He is not a loving savior and an unloving lord. He is one person. The unity of Jesus is why Paul also described salvation through making a solemn profession in the Lord Jesus. Romans 10:9 is also translated, "That if you confess with your mouth Jesus *as* Lord" (NASB). We are saved by calling on Jesus in faith, recognizing who he is: the Lord.

Until you receive God's salvation by making this kind of repentant-faith commitment to Jesus, you cannot be prosperous or successful in pursuing God's plan for your life. Jesus promises that those who are in him "will bear much fruit," but apart from Jesus, "you can do nothing" (John 15:5). Believing in Jesus is the first step in the path of pursuing success.

---

1.  NIV: "For they loved human praise more than praise from God." The NIV uses the word "praise" instead of "glory," but in the original Greek, it is the same word, δοξα.

---

## ∾ CHAPTER 4 ∾

# UNDERSTANDING YOUR WEAKNESSES WHILE PURSUING SUCCESS

---

> Let us throw off everything that hinders and the
> sin that so easily entangles. And let us run with
> perseverance the race marked out for us.
>
> —Hebrews 12:1

If God has saved us, why is it that sin still "so easily entangles" us? If we are going to run with perseverance the race to glorify God in our lives and be prosperous and successful, we need an answer to that question. We need to know our weaknesses. When God saves us, he does many things that change us in helpful ways. He sets us "free from sin" (Romans 6:18) and comes into our hearts through the Holy Spirit (Galatians 4:6). Yet, God also tells us that there is more to do. Our salvation is not yet complete.

Paul wrote to the Romans that believers in Jesus have not yet experienced all that we can in our new relationship with Jesus. We have received our salvation in part but not in full. "We ourselves, who have the firstfruits of the Spirit, groan inwardly as we wait eagerly for our adoption to sonship, the redemption of our bodies" (Romans 8:23). There is a groaning in response to ongoing pain in our life. The pain is a result of ongoing effects of sin in our physical bodies. We have not yet experienced redemption.

Think about how God could have done things. He could have made it so that the moment we believe in Jesus, our salvation would be complete. We would instantly receive bodies entirely free from the effects of sin. The most noticeable difference would be that we would not die. Death is a consequence of sin. The fact that believers in Jesus still die means that some aspect of sin is still with us, still impacting us. That will not always be the case. Paul wrote, "And if the Spirit of him who raised Jesus from the dead is living in you, he who raised Christ from the dead will also give life to your mortal bodies" (Romans 8:11). This is something the Spirit *will* do, meaning he has not yet done it.

In addition to death, the presence of sin in our physical bodies means that believers still struggle against sin. Paul added, "If by the Spirit you put to death the misdeeds of the body, you will live" (Romans 8:13). Paul wrote this in the present tense, emphasizing that it is an ongoing process in the life of the believer. He assumes everyone who has the Spirit present in their life will keep putting to death the misdeeds of the body, leading to eternal life. Paul put it this way in Romans 6:22: "But now that you have been set free from sin and have become slaves of God, the benefit you reap leads to holiness, and the result is eternal life." Notice that two things are true about those who are saved: We are both free from sin but not yet fully holy. We have a benefit that "leads to holiness," but we have not yet arrived.

So we continue to face death and struggle with sin. We also suffer. We suffer physical aches and pains as our bodies decline and move toward death. We suffer physically because of the harsh conditions of the natural world that we are exposed to as a result of the Fall. We also suffer emotionally because of sin. This may be the result of our own sin and sinful attitudes or because of sin committed against us by others. Sin is ultimately behind worry, depression, fear, and anger.

Since God will end our suffering one day as part of his gift of salvation to us, why does he wait? Why doesn't he do it now? The Bible does not give us the complete answer to this question, but it tells us that there is one. The Bible says that it is necessary for believers in Jesus to continue to suffer in order to bring about our future glory. The glory is the full salvation we will receive one day when we will be completely free from death, suffering, and the struggle with sin in our physical bodies. Paul wrote, "Now if we are children, then we are heirs—heirs of God and co-heirs with Christ, if indeed we share in his sufferings in order that we may also share in his glory" (Romans 8:17). Suffering is necessary to achieve something. Paul added good news about what the suffering will accomplish: "I consider that our present sufferings are not worth comparing with the glory that will be revealed in us" (Romans 8:18).

## Body and Spirit

Why does the Bible say there is still sin in our physical bodies while maintaining that we are free from sin? The answer is that every person has both a physical body and a spirit. While each of us is one person made of body and spirit, it is possible for the spiritual, nonmaterial aspect of us to separate from the body. Paul wrote that he would "prefer to be away from the body and at home with the Lord" (2 Corinthians 4:8). He meant that when a believer's physical body dies, the nonmaterial spirit goes on to live with Jesus. We will still exist, have consciousness, and be aware of who we are and what is going on around us.

However, we will not live in heaven forever without a body. In the future, our physical bodies will be raised to life and changed in glorious ways. At that time, the spirit that lives in heaven will be reunited with a body. Those who are still physically alive when the resurrection occurs will immediately receive a glorified body. Paul wrote, "We will not all sleep, but we will all be changed—in a flash in the twinkling of an eye, at the last trumpet. For the trumpet will sound, the dead will be raised imperishable, and we will be changed" (1 Corinthians 15:51–52).

Paul referred to both the physical body and spiritual aspect of humanity when he wrote about salvation in Romans 6–8. At salvation, the believer's spiritual self, the nonmaterial inner person, is freed from the power of sin. Paul wrote that "we know that our old self was crucified with him [Jesus] so that the body ruled by sin might be done away with, that we should no longer be slaves to sin" (Romans 6:6). Now, clearly the physical body was not literally crucified with Jesus. Christians do not have wounds appear in their wrists and feet when they believe in Jesus. Paul is saying that in some sense, when Jesus was crucified, the one who believes in Jesus was also crucified—not the physical body but the spirit. When he died, we (who were under the power of sin) died. Then we were given new life (Romans 6:4). Through this process, we are now no longer under the power of sin.

Paul continued by saying that believers should now "count yourselves dead to sin but alive to God in Christ Jesus" (Romans 6:11). In our nonmaterial spirit, we are free from sin. However, Paul immediately added, "Therefore do not let sin reign in your mortal body so that you obey its evil desires" (Romans 6:12). So while we are free from the power of sin in our spirit, we still have evil desires in our "mortal body." Our inner, spiritual self has power over sin, but sinful desires are still present with the physical body we remain attached to.

The fact that Paul commanded believers to "not let sin reign in your mortal body so that you obey its evil desires" must mean that it is at least possible for a believer to obey evil desires. Paul would have no reason to prohibit something that a believer is not even capable of doing. He gives this urgent command because he knows that sin is a danger for the believer. Paul's command tells us that if a believer is not actively fighting against sin in the mortal body, it will regain dangerous influence in the believer's life.

However, Paul's command to keep sin from reigning also means that Christians can succeed in the fight against sin. Paul would not have commanded Christians to fight sin if they had no chance of success. That would be like commanding believers to jump to the moon. No, the fact that Paul gives this command indicates that both responses to sin are possible. A Christian can either fall into the dangers of sin or refuse to obey its evil desires.

## Pursuing the Goal with Our Thinking

The Joshua 1:8 promise tells us that the path to being prosperous and successful requires changing our thinking. We must fight sin in order to keep moving toward the goal of glorifying God with our lives. The path to success is the same as a path to holiness. Joshua 1:8 says we will only be successful when we study the Bible and "meditate on it day and night." Only then can we carefully "do everything written in it." We meditate on the Bible so our thinking lines up with biblical teaching.

Romans 6:11 also tells us that changing our thinking is the key to success. Paul described how to fight sin: "Count yourselves dead to sin but alive to God." Fighting sin is a battle in the mind. We fight sin as we count ourselves dead to it. We count ourselves dead to sin because that is the truth. In Christ, we are dead to sin. However, we must continue to consider what happened at the cross. We must recount Jesus's death and resurrection and how it relates to the change in our own lives. We must meditate on it, day and night, or we may soon live as if we are under the power of sin.

Changing our thinking is a continual process. Paul commanded Christians to "be transformed by the renewing of your mind" (Romans 12:2). It is not enough to learn about Jesus at one time. We need to renew understanding, again and again. Jesus said his disciples must "take up their cross daily" (Luke 9:23). Since it is impossible for a person to literally be crucified every day, he could not have been referring to physical crucifixion. He was speaking about a spiritual act. Every day, believers must consider themselves crucified with Christ and no longer living, but having Christ living in them (Galatians 2:20). The goal of right thinking is not about interpreting circumstances in a more positive way, a sort of intense pretending. Instead, believers are to maintain a proper understanding of what is true about their circumstances because of what God has done. Without daily renewal, believers will revert to acting in a way that is not in line with who they really are.[1]

Paul also described the battle of the mind in 2 Corinthians 10:5: "We demolish arguments and every pretension that sets itself up against the knowledge of God, and we take captive every thought to make it obedient to Christ." The battle of the mind involves growing in knowledge of God. Every thought must line up with what is true about God. A distorted view of God will result in a distorted view of our circumstances and the proper way to pursue our goal of glorifying him. Our fight against sin necessarily includes studying the Bible to learn about God.

The good news is that the Bible has everything we need to win this fight for right thinking. Paul wrote, "All Scripture is God-breathed and is useful for teaching, rebuking, correcting and training in righteousness, so that the servant of God may be thoroughly equipped for every good work" (2 Timothy 3:16–17). There is nothing about our thinking that needs to change for us to be prosperous and successful that is not addressed sufficiently in the Bible. The more we meditate on God's Word, the more we will be "thoroughly equipped for every good work." We will be able to "carefully do everything written in it" (Joshua 1:8).

## Pursuing the Goal with Our Behavior

Both Joshua 1:8 and 2 Timothy 3:17 draw a connection between thinking and doing. If we are meditating on Scripture in the right way, we will also change our behavior. Our fight against sin begins with thinking, but we must also focus on doing. Meditating on the Bible is necessary, "so that you may be careful to do everything written in it" (Joshua 1:8). The Bible is useful for us because it prepares us to do "every good work" (2 Timothy 3:17).

Thinking and doing are also combined in Ephesians 4:22–25: "You were taught, with regard to your former way of life, to put off your old self, which is being corrupted by its deceitful desires; to be made new in the attitude of your minds; and to put on the new self, created to be like God in true righteousness and holiness. Therefore each of you must put off falsehood and speak truthfully to your neighbor." In this text, Paul first emphasized the need to change our thinking when he urged us "to be made new in the attitude of your minds" in order to overcome "deceitful desires." He then shifted to behavior, calling on believers to "put off your old self" and "put on the new self." We are to "put on ... true righteousness and holiness."

As we renew the mind, we will live in increasing righteousness, the way we are designed to live. This shows up in visible ways. Paul gave an immediate example: "You must put off falsehood and speak truthfully" (Ephesians 4:25). As thinking changes, sinful behaviors like lying will be replaced with righteous behaviors like speaking truthfully.

Paul added another example of putting off sin and putting on righteousness a few verses later. He addressed a person in the church in Ephesus who had been stealing. He told him to stop stealing. That is the "put off" command. But Paul didn't stop there. He added that the thief "must work, doing something useful with their own hands, that they may have something to share with those in need" (Ephesians 4:28). Paul understood that the thief would have greater success in changing his sinful pattern of stealing when he started working to give to others.

Paul was revealing an important strategy for overcoming sin in our life. We cannot simply stop the sin. We need to find a new, righteous behavior to replace it with. We will have greater success over sinful behaviors in our lives when we add corresponding righteous behaviors. For a thief, that means starting to share generously with others. For other sins, there are other matching righteous behaviors to develop.

After the resurrection, Jesus defined the ongoing mission for all his followers. He called on them to "go and make disciples of all nations." Then he described a two-step process for making disciples. The first step is to baptize a new believer. The second step is "teaching them to obey everything I have commanded you" (Matthew 28:19–20). Teaching addresses thinking because information is being passed from the teacher to the student. However, just as we have seen in

Joshua 1:8 and in Paul's writing, biblical teaching does not only address thinking. Jesus said that teaching should lead to changes in behavior. The goal of teaching is to lead disciples to obey everything Jesus commanded.

Jesus called all his followers to be part of this kind of disciple making. That means all believers in Jesus want to live out the Joshua 1:8 promise to meditate on biblical commands and carefully do them. They also work to help others begin and grow in this journey. Aligning thinking and behavior with biblical teaching is the path to being prosperous and successful.

## Modern Psychology and Success

Modern psychology also focuses on how to help people change. People seek help from a therapist because there is something they don't like about themselves. They are hurting because of various types of emotional pain or destructive behavior. They want to feel or act differently. They may seek counseling because of a drug addiction, depression, anxiety, panic attacks, an eating disorder, or one of many other burdens that are weighing them down in life. No one visits a therapist to say, "I feel great and love how my life is going right now." Secular counseling tries to find a way to help people make the changes they want to make in their lives without using a religious source like the Bible. Secular psychologists seek to apply principles of science to study human behavior and identify effective ways to help people change.

Beginning in the late 1800s, Sigmund Freud advanced a number of ideas that shaped the development of modern psychology. His ideas are known as psychoanalysis. Freud focused on unconscious thoughts and the interpretation of dreams. He theorized that mental problems are the result of an overactive conscience and feelings of guilt. Dreams and other types of guided talking sessions could provide insight into the hidden world of the unconscious. There, the psychoanalyst could expect to find inner tensions about controlling or embracing certain urges that begin in childhood. Freud rejected the idea of real guilt. Overcoming mental problems was a matter of helping people remove their false sense of guilt.[2]

Notice that this is a very different approach to success than what the Bible teaches. Jesus said those who are "weary and burdened" should come to him for rest (Matthew 11:28), where "coming to Jesus" means seeking to learn and obey his teaching. Jesus preached that people should repent from sin and find forgiveness in him. Jesus did not say to go to an expert in psychoanalysis to help you understand your unconscious thoughts so that you can learn to not feel guilty anymore. Jesus directed people to find a solution to the real problem of guilt by receiving the forgiveness that can only be found in him. Can both of these different ideas about the path to success be right? No, because they contradict each other in fundamental ways.

Later in the twentieth century, secular counseling techniques began to shift away from Freudian psychoanalysis to newer approaches. Experience did not demonstrate that Freud's techniques were really helping people at a sufficient level. Psychologists began to propose a variety of methods for helping people overcome problems in life. Countless studies have evaluated the effectiveness of each new approach. Each study sought to determine the percentage of people who were able to overcome significant problems through the counseling they receive. The studies are useful for comparing the effectiveness of different strategies. Over time, psychologists have developed strategies that have an increasing ability to show measurable results. Today, out of the various secular strategies that have been tried, there is a growing consensus that cognitive behavioral therapy (CBT) offers the best help for the majority of counseling problems.

## Cognitive Behavioral Therapy

What is cognitive behavioral therapy? It is a combination of two earlier counseling strategies. Cognitive therapy focuses on changing thinking. Behavioral therapy focuses on changing behavior. Initially developed to help people struggling with depression, CBT prescribes addressing emotional problems by addressing a counselee's thinking and behavior patterns. A depressed person may have certain negative thoughts that come up again and again that are not true or come from an overly pessimistic perspective. Such thoughts become habits or automatic responses. They may think, "I'm a failure," or "I can't do anything right," so often that they can no longer control it or respond with a more accurate assessment. A cognitive behavioral therapist will work to help the counselee learn to interpret events in a more helpful way.[3]

The therapist will also encourage new behaviors to help the depressed person become more active. They will help the counselee set goals to do things like "initiate new friendships and spend more time with current friends."[4] Changing behavior is a key component in helping to change thoughts. The assumption is that the emotional pain of depression will decrease as new thoughts and behaviors replace the old ones.

Cognitive behavioral therapists have developed counseling strategies for many other types of psychiatric disorders, including anxiety, obsessive-compulsive disorder, and eating disorders. Hundreds of studies have demonstrated that this is an effective treatment method. As early as 1977, a study revealed that CBT was as effective in treating depression as a common antidepressant medication. Since then, studies have even demonstrated that therapy causes observable neurobiological changes.[5]

## Cognitive Behavioral Therapy and the Bible

What does this have to do with the Bible? First, I believe that research supporting CBT provides additional evidence that we can trust the Bible to guide us to success. Modern psychologists have experimented with different techniques and conducted studies for more than a century to try to learn how to help hurting people. In the end, they have "discovered" strategies that the Bible taught all along. The Bible has always maintained that addressing underlying thinking and behavioral patterns is a key to solving emotional problems. The Bible demonstrates an intimate knowledge of human psychology that is easy to explain only when one recognizes a divine origin. As our creator, God knows exactly how we are designed to function properly and shares that knowledge in verse after verse.

Hebrews 4:12 says, "The word of God is alive and active. Sharper than any double-edged sword, it penetrates even to dividing soul and spirit, joints and marrow; it judges the thoughts and attitudes of the heart." The Bible claims to have amazing insights into the human heart. That is good news because it means that the Bible can help us with our deepest struggles. As a counselor, I can tell you that I have personally seen God work through his Word in powerful ways to help people with all sorts of issues that we usually call mental illness.

The Bible is essentially a counseling manual, telling us what we need to know in order to make changes in our lives that are for our good. We may think we don't have a mental health problem, but that really depends on what a mental health problem is. The standards and definitions of different mental health disorders that psychologists turn to today are found in the *Diagnostic and Statistical Manual of Mental Disorders*. The specific symptoms required for a particular diagnosis are spelled out in detail. For instance, a diagnosis of "Major Depressive Episode" requires the presence of at least five symptoms out of a list of nine. The list includes problems like "depressed mood most of the day," "markedly diminished interest or pleasure in all, or almost all, activities most of the day," and "insomnia or hypersomnia nearly every day."[6]

But checking off the items on the list does not guarantee a diagnosis. There are other considerations. Most noteworthy is this qualification: "The symptoms cause clinically significant distress or impairment in social, occupational, or other important areas of functioning."[7] The threshold of a mental illness is whether a counselee is functioning or not. Is the person unable to hold a job or maintain relationships because of depression? If so, she or he meets the criteria of a mental health disorder. This standard holds true for most diagnosable disorders. Every person may exhibit one, a few, or half a dozen symptoms of any particular mental illness. A particular symptom may be mild or intense. There are a lot of gray areas as to whether a person has a particular disorder. Even the issue of "functioning" is a difficult concept to pin down precisely.

In reality, all of us struggle to some extinct with the symptoms associated with one or more mental health problems, even though most problems don't rise to the level of a diagnosis. We all have weaknesses. We live in physical bodies that endure the negative effects of sin. We all have harmful thinking patterns, behaviors, addictions, or emotional pain inflicted on us by other sinful people. The Bible understands our weaknesses and the best way to work toward overcoming them, because the Bible comes from a caring God who knows every intimate detail about us.

Every one of us needs counseling if we are going to be prosperous and successful in life. We may not need to make an appointment with a counselor, but we need counseling. The Bible is the resource we should turn to for counseling. The extensive research demonstrating the effectiveness of CBT should increase our confidence that the Bible is the ultimate resource for life. The data confirms the effectiveness of the biblical approach to solving emotional and behavioral problems. In addition, the Bible offers a counseling resource that is superior to CBT in many ways.

## How the Bible Is Superior to Cognitive Behavioral Therapy

Let's begin by looking at how the Bible deals with a specific counseling problem like depression. Both the Bible and CBT propose that false, inaccurate, or incomplete thoughts that have become ingrained in the individual need to change. Both seek to identify what those thoughts are and replace them with new thoughts. The Bible has something to say about every damaging thought that may run through the mind of a depressed person. The Bible tells us that we are created by a loving God who designed us for a special purpose (Isaiah 43:7). God is always with us and has even endured unimaginable costs to provide us with forgiveness (Psalm 23, John 3:16). The God of the whole universe even wants us to be full of joy (Philippians 4:4). These are just a few of the encouraging concepts the Bible offers.

Like CBT, the Bible acknowledges that simply hearing these wonderful truths will not usually bring about the desired relief from depression. As Joshua 1:8 says, we must "meditate on it day and night." We have to work at our thinking, replacing unbiblical thoughts with biblical ones. The unbiblical thoughts may be ingrained in us because we have thought them so often, but change is possible.

The Bible and CBT also address behavior as one of the important components for changing thinking. There are many instances where the Bible prescribes behavioral therapy to bring relief to depression. For example, Isaiah 58:10 says, "If you spend yourselves in behalf of the hungry and satisfy the needs of the oppressed, then your light will rise in the darkness and your night will become like the noonday." People with depression may improve their inward and negative thoughts about life by volunteering to help others in need. CBT would call this becoming "active." It is a biblical concept.

What about medical treatments for depression? There are still more questions than answers when it comes to a medical understanding of depression and other mental illnesses. In a small percentage of cases, there are medical conditions that cause the symptoms associated with depression. In other cases, there may be some physical illness that is not yet understood. There can also be physical factors that contribute to depression that are not necessarily illnesses, such as lack of sleep, poor diet, and inadequate exercise. Sometimes, medication can help alleviate the symptoms of depression, but often it does not, and it may cause other unwanted side effects. Anyone who struggles with depression should have a medical examination to check for possible physical contributing factors.

Both the Bible and CBT acknowledge a separate but important role for the medical community in addressing mental illness. The Bible tells us that doctors have a role to play in treating those who are sick (Matthew 9:12), while recognizing that doctors have limitations (Mark 5:26). Because the Bible teaches that people have a physical and spiritual nature, we should not ignore either one when addressing mental illness.

The Bible says so much about the wide variety of difficulties we face in life. As a counselor, I take time to listen and understand the problems in each situation. Then I turn to the Bible to develop a specific strategy to help. There is always a sufficient amount of assistance in the Bible to address counseling needs. Although I could offer helpful counsel without using the Bible, I would be at a significant disadvantage. Modern psychologists have made a lot of progress in developing CBT, but the Bible offers far more. The Bible provides superior counsel for at least six reasons:

## 1. The Bible has authority to evaluate the right goals for people.

In CBT, goals are oriented around helping people function better, which means holding a job and maintaining social relationships. The Bible has a richer and more comprehensive perspective on goals. The Bible proclaims that we are a special part of God's creation and are designed to enjoy seeking God and his glory. Biblical counseling not only identifies the main goal in life; it also provides instruction on the types of goals that will help us succeed in reaching the ultimate goal. Many people simply don't know what they are supposed to be living for. That is one of the thinking problems the Bible addresses. The Bible helps counselees pursue something better in life than what they even realize they want.

Steve Jobs held a similar concept as a business leader. He once explained that Apple did not develop technology by asking consumers what they want. He said, "A lot of times, people don't know what they want until you show it to them."[8] He believed Apple could make products that people didn't realize they wanted until after they saw them. Similarly, counseling from the Bible reveals what a counselee's goals should be based on what a loving God says on the matter. Only Bible-based counseling will emphasize goals like holiness and pursuing a relationship with the living God.[9] This is the only thing that will bring true peace and joy in life. CBT, on the other hand, allows counselees to decide what goals they want to pursue in life and settles for goals related to functioning.

## 2. The Bible establishes what is true.

CBT guides counselees to change thinking and behaviors in ways that help with behavioral and emotional problems. But CBT cannot evaluate if a behavior or thought is right or wrong. Only the Bible has authority behind every truth claim that is proclaimed, every goal that is mandated, and every behavior that is commanded.

In the specific example of depression, both the Bible and CBT seek to identify automatic thinking patterns that are overly pessimistic. Counselees may believe that life is no longer worth living because there is nothing worth doing or pursuing. I might try to help them change their thinking, but how do I know that what they are thinking isn't actually true? CBT methods encourage them to think more positively about their situation. But how does CBT know that the counselee is wrong? CBT has no basis for assuring them that a more positive view is true.

But the Bible tells me that every person is created in God's image and is loved by the God of the entire universe. God loves each one of us so much that he demonstrated it by sending Jesus to pay for our sins. Therefore, each human being has immense value and worth. I know this because God has revealed it. Therefore, as I counsel from the Bible, I have a basis to help people believe truth that is helpful. No matter what the circumstances, counselees have reason to be optimistic about their value and purpose. Outside of the Bible, I have no foundation from which to assure them of this outlook.

## 3. CBT has nothing to say about the sovereignty and goodness of God, which is so important to helpful thinking.

We understand ourselves and our purpose only when we know about the one who created us and have confidence that he has complete control and good intentions behind everything he does. How else can we prosper and succeed while facing the brutal pain of a health crises or financial disaster? Secular CBT counseling is not able to help counselees believe these truths about God. In subsequent chapters, I will show how the Bible provides answers to these issues.

## 4. CBT cannot counsel on the role of prayer or the Holy Spirit in overcoming problems.

Only the Bible gives us all the necessary information we need to effectively understand and address the continuing problems in our thinking and behaviors.

## 5. The Bible gets deeper than thinking; it addresses the heart.

CBT is limited in that it maintains that bad thinking is the root of all psychological distress. The Bible recognizes that thinking is important, but desires and affections of the heart are at a deeper level and more fundamental to our problems. Although CBT approaches a biblical model of counseling, it does not start with the same assumptions about what a human being is, and therefore it falls short of the level of care the Bible offers. Our problems are not only mental, but mental and spiritual. Each person is made of body and spirit. Only God working through his powerful Word can bring about the spiritual change that leads to changes in our thinking (Hebrews 4:12). The Bible gets to the deepest level of human problems.[10]

## 6. Only the Bible helps with the greatest need of every person.

CBT may help people feel better, but it cannot do anything to remove sin and guilt before God. The Bible explains that the only way to start moving on the path to true success is by receiving forgiveness through faith in Jesus Christ. CBT can offer temporary relief from some of life's challenging problems, but only the Bible gives answers for life's greatest problem.

### Using the Bible to Pursue Success

The call to follow Jesus is a call to become more prosperous and successful by aligning our thinking and behavior with biblical teaching. As Christians, we have assurance that God has forgiven our sin, given us power over sin, and given us many wonderful promises about eternal life. However, we still have weaknesses. Our physical body continues to endure the effects of sin, as evident in sickness and death. Because we are attached to our physical bodies, we still have sinful attitudes, thoughts, and behaviors. God has allowed this to continue, for his own good purposes.

The Bible addresses our thinking and behavior in ways that will lead us to be more prosperous and successful. We will never eradicate the painful effects of sin on our physical bodies in this lifetime. However, we can find increasing joy, peace, and a love for life as we learn to meditate on God's Word day and night and carefully do everything written in it. In the remaining chapters of this book, I will address critical areas the Bible calls us to consider in our thinking and behavior in order to have a prosperous and successful life.

## For Further Reading

Hodges, Charles D. *Good Mood, Bad Mood.* Wapwallopen, PA: Shepherd Press, 2012.

Lambert, Heath. *A Theology of Biblical Counseling.* Grand Rapids, MI: Zondervan, 2016.

The Institute for Biblical Counseling & Discipleship, "Free Resources." https://ibcd.org/resources/

---

1. Charles Leiter, *Justification and Regeneration* (Muscle Shoals, AL: HeartCry Resources, 2007), 87.
2. Jay E. Adams, *Competent to Counsel* (Grand Rapids, MI: Zondervan, 1970), 10.
3. Judith S. Beck, *Cognitive Behavior Therapy,* 2nd ed. (Guilford, NY, 2011), 7.
4. Ibid., 8.
5. Ibid., 4–5.
6. Charles D. Hodges, *Good Mood, Bad Mood* (Wapwallopen, PA: Shepherd Press, 2012), 26.
7. Ibid.
8. *BusinessWeek* (May 25, 1998).
9. Scott Mehl, "The CBT Therapist in Us All." In *ACBC Essays*, Vol. 1 (2017), 37.
10. Nate Brooks, "Is Biblical Counseling Really CBT?" accessed August 13, 2018. https://biblicalcounseling.com/2018/06/is-biblical-counseling-really-cbt/

## CHAPTER 5

# UNDERSTANDING GOD'S POWER WHILE PURSUING SUCCESS

You intended to harm me, but God intended it for good to accomplish what is now being done, the saving of many lives.

—Genesis 50:20

Joseph is one of the Bible's great success stories. The first thing the Bible tells us about Joseph is that he had eleven brothers from four different mothers—and all four were married to his father, Jacob, at the same time. Imagine if they had reality TV back then. Joseph was number eleven, and his mother Rachel was Jacob's favorite wife.

The oldest brothers felt entitled to a prominent role in the future of the family. They believed their father was unfairly passing this role down to their little brother because he had the favored mother. Jacob's polygamous family arrangement was never approved by God, and the story itself explains why. Obviously, the situation caused a great deal of turmoil between Joseph and his brothers.

The family owned many sheep and goats. The ten older brothers would stay with the flock, sometimes traveling miles from home. When Joseph was seventeen, Jacob sent him to check on his brothers. Filled with jealousy, the brothers attacked him and plotted to kill him. Eventually, they decided to sell him to slave traders on the way to Egypt instead (Genesis 37). Why waste an opportunity to make a buck?

Slave traders hauled Joseph away, and he assumed he would never see his home or father again. Twenty years passed before Joseph had the opportunity to confront his brothers. By that time, Joseph had experienced many ups and downs. He had risen to the highest position in a wealthy Egyptian household, only to be thrown into prison for a life sentence. The charges brought against him were completely false. He was eventually exonerated and rose to the second highest position in all Egypt, the most powerful kingdom on earth at the time. When his brothers came to Egypt looking to purchase grain, they knew nothing about the Egyptian ruler's true identity.

Joseph could have done anything he wanted to his brothers, who had treated him so terribly. But Joseph forgave them, wept when he was reunited with them, and provided for all their needs. Where his brothers failed to control their anger and jealously, Joseph possessed an amazing ability to pursue a different path. The Bible points to his character and faith in God as the reason he was able to thrive even in the midst of great suffering and mistreatment. Joseph showed a way out of the cloud of bitterness that seeks after every victim of physical and sexual abuse, bullying, violence, and injustice.

At the moment Joseph's brothers thought he was going to get his revenge against them, Joseph revealed the secret of his success to them. He urged them not to be afraid. Then he explained, "You intended to harm me, but God intended it for good to accomplish what is now being done, the saving of many lives" (Genesis 50:20). Joseph acknowledged that they did wrong, but he also knew that God was behind the events in his life. He believed that God is good and directs all things for a good purpose.

Joseph knew that many people would have starved if he had not come to Egypt and become a great leader. Joseph trusted that God knew what he was doing and that God demonstrated kindness in and through the suffering he endured. Joseph's perspective gave him the strength to keep pursuing the right goal in life (glorifying God), even in the midst of what would seem like devastating setbacks to most of us.

But what, exactly, was Joseph saying? In what way did God intend for his brothers to attack him? Did God cause it or simply allow it? Did he make the brothers do what they did? Were his brothers even guilty of sin if they were only doing what God had planned all along? We may be happy for Joseph that he was able to take such tragic events in stride and keep serving God. However, when we are in the midst of pain, God often seems far away. What about when a child is killed in a car accident by a drunk driver, or when an angry husband beats his wife? What about natural evil like cancer? Does God intend that, as Joseph believed about his trials?

The problem of evil is probably the single greatest reason people lose their faith in God. The argument is that:

1.  If God is loving, he will want to stop pain and evil.
2.  If God is all–powerful, he is able to stop pain and evil.
3.  But pain and evil exist.
4.  Therefore, God is either not loving or not able to stop pain and evil. God, at least the way the Bible describes him, must not exist.

Even among believers, this line of thinking causes doubts about God's presence in the midst of suffering. While believers may not openly question God's goodness or his power as a result of evil, they still often fall short of being able to declare boldly, as Joseph did, that God "intended it for good." From Joseph's perspective, the evil he endured was actually a demonstration of God's love and power. Learning to see life the way Joseph did is a foundational concept the Bible teaches so that we can be prosperous and successful. Understanding God's love and power is one of the ways we come to Jesus to find rest (Matthew 11:28).

So what did Joseph mean by the phrase, "God intended it for good"? Joseph had a lot of time while he was in slavery and in prison to think about the events that led to his brothers' betrayal. He knew that God could have intervened and stopped the brothers from doing what they did in any number of ways. However, Joseph understood that God's involvement was not merely a passive choice to allow the brothers' actions to go forward. Joseph said that God "intended it." He believed God actually planned this event. I think he was able to identify three specific ways that God's actions led to the greatest pain in his life, a pain he eventually thanked God for.

## How God Did It

Genesis 37 reveals each of the three ways that God accomplished his good purposes through the wicked actions of Joseph's brothers. First, God caused the birth order of the twelve brothers. The Bible says that Jacob "loved Joseph more than any of his other sons, because he had been born to him in his old age" (Genesis 37:3). The Bible also tells us that the reason the brothers hated Joseph was because their father loved him more (Genesis 37:4). Jacob's preferential treatment of Joseph was no coincidence. Genesis 29 and 30 describe how God directly caused the birth order that led to Jacob's feelings toward Joseph.

Jacob married Leah and Rachel in consecutive weeks. Yet Leah had six different sons, while Rachel was unable to get pregnant. The Bible explains, "When the LORD saw that Leah was not loved, he enabled her to conceive, but Rachel remained childless" (Genesis 29:31). The text repeats that God was behind Leah's impressive fertility streak as she continued to have more children. When Rachel finally gave birth to her firstborn son, Joseph, the Bible tells us this was because "God remembered Rachel; he listened to her and enabled her to conceive" (Genesis 30:22). Therefore, God's actions led to the situation that provoked Joseph's brothers to jealousy.

However, that is not all God did. Joseph also had a dream, which he described to his brothers. The Bible says the brothers then "hated him all the more" (Genesis 37:5) because they realized it was a prophecy about a future time when they would bow down to Joseph (Genesis 37:7). We know that this was no ordinary dream. In fact,

God sent the dream. We know this because everything prophesied in the dream came to pass. Many years later, when Joseph was made a ruler over Egypt, the brothers did bow down to Joseph. God sent this dream to Joseph knowing that it would provoke the brothers to even greater jealousy of Joseph.

Finally, God intervened a third time by sending an unusual man to guide Joseph to his brothers on the very day they betrayed him. Earlier that day, Joseph's father sent him to check on the older brothers who were watching flocks in Shechem. However, Joseph didn't find them in Shechem. Instead, a man "found him wandering around in the fields and asked him, "What are you looking for?" (Genesis 37:15). Notice that Joseph didn't meet the man while he was going around asking people if anyone saw his brothers. The man came to Joseph. The man then told Joseph to go to Dothan, and when he arrived in Dothan, his brothers seized him and plotted to kill him.

If the man hadn't sought Joseph out and told him about his brothers, Joseph would have never found them. In addition, because he encountered the brothers at Dothan, rather than Shechem, he was thrown into a cistern along a major trade route. This provided the occasion for the brothers to sell Joseph into slavery and for Joseph to eventually become the ruler of Egypt. If the brothers caught him at Shechem, they probably would have killed him.

The Bible could have left all of these details out of the story and simply reported that Joseph found his brothers in Dothan. However, the Bible included this part of the story so we would again see God at work in Joseph's betrayal. The appearance of an unusual and unidentified man at precisely the right time was no coincidence. God was behind the man's appearance. Joseph realized this as well. As he toiled in slavery and later was in anguish in prison because of a false accusation, he could have spent all his time fantasizing about getting revenge on his brothers. Instead, he thought about the events that led to his suffering and reasoned that God intended it. He also concluded that God had a good purpose for intending it.

# Does God Cause Sin?

If God intended for Joseph's brothers to brutally assault him and sell him into slavery, did the brothers have any choice in the matter? Did God make them do evil? For that matter, does God make every murderer, adulterer, and rapist do it? Certainly not. God is not a moral monster. Yet, God does *intend* it. It is part of his plan. God directs evil in a way that accomplishes his good purposes. Understanding how he does this is fundamental to understanding how to pursue prosperity and success the way Joseph did.

Look back at Genesis 50:20. Notice that Joseph does not say that God was the only one who intended it. He also says the brothers intended to harm him. "You intended to harm me, but God intended it for good." Joseph does not excuse their behavior or suggest they are not responsible for their actions. It was their own wicked hearts that led them to extreme jealousy and hatred of their brother. It was their own evil desires that led them to attack their brother. They chose to do what they did, and they were guilty for their actions.

Joseph must have understood that God's actions were based on his knowledge of what the brothers would do in certain circumstances. In fact, none of the actions that God took to bring about the events in Genesis 37 make sense unless God knew what would happen as a result. God knew that Jacob would love the son of his favorite wife Rachel more than the other brothers. He knew that having Joseph born after the others would cause jealousy. He knew sending the dream would lead to Joseph sharing the dream and the brothers hating him even more. He knew this not because he was controlling or manipulating them, but because he knew the evil that was already in their hearts. He knew exactly what would happen that fateful day if he got word to Joseph that the brothers went to Dothan.

The brothers could have acted differently, but God knew that they would not. God knows everything about the future. David exclaimed, "Before a word is on my tongue you, LORD, know it completely" (Psalm 139:4). God knows what people will do before they do it. That does not mean that God necessarily causes them to do things, only that he knows what they will do.

For example, imagine you watch a recorded football game with your friend. Your friend saw the game last night, but you didn't. You are excited when your team wins the game with a last-second touchdown. Your friend knew exactly what was going to happen because he already saw the game. Does this mean your friend caused your team to win the game? Should you thank him for giving your team the victory? Of course not; he simply knew what would happen.

However, God's knowledge of the future goes beyond this. He knows more than what will happen. He knows what would happen in every possible scenario. Going back to the football game, God doesn't simply know who will win the football game and how; he knows who would have won the game in every possible scenario. Would there have been a different outcome if the weather was ten degrees warmer and the wind was five mile per hour faster? God knows the answer to questions like that, and he also has the ability to influence the weather (and an infinite number of other things).

## God's Knowledge and Control

God's knowledge of what would happen in different circumstances is illustrated in 1 Samuel 23. At the time, Saul was king over Israel, and he was jealous of a rising political star, a military hero named David. Saul thought he had an opportunity to kill David, who was staying in a town called Keilah. "Saul was told that David had gone to Keilah, and he said, 'God has delivered him into my hands, for David has imprisoned himself by entering a town with gates and bars'" (1 Samuel 23:7).

David responded by asking God for information about what he should do next. God revealed to David that Saul was going to come to Keilah (1 Samuel 23:11). Once David knew that Saul was coming, he wanted to know what the citizens of Keilah would do when Saul arrived. He needed to know if he should stay in the city and trust their protection, or if he needed to flee the city because they would hand him over to Saul. Fleeing would come with risk, so he needed to know what would happen in each scenario. It was a life-and-death decision.

So he asked God, "'Will the citizens of Keilah surrender me and my men to Saul?' And the LORD said, 'They will'" (1 Samuel 23:12). Of course, David didn't wait around to see God's words come true. The next verse reports, "So David and his men, about six hundred in number, left Keilah and kept moving" (1 Samuel 23:13). Before Saul ever made it to Keilah, he heard that David had left, and so he canceled his trip to Keilah and never made it there.

This story reveals God's comprehensive knowledge about both the future and the potential future. God knew that Saul would have come to Keilah if David had remained there. He knew that the citizens of Keilah would have handed David over to Saul if David had stayed there. David responded to this information by leaving, so the citizens of Keilah never had the opportunity to actually hand David over. But God knew what would have happened if David had stayed. God not only knows what will happen in the future but also what would happen in the future in different circumstances.[1]

In this instance, God shared with David what would happen if he stayed in Keilah, so David also had knowledge of potential future events. David then used that knowledge to choose which events would actually take place. Given the choice between staying in Keilah and being captured by Saul and leaving to avoid that outcome, David chose to leave.

Although the citizens of Keilah never knew it, David made the decision about whether they would hand him over to Saul. Had he decided to stay in Keilah, they would have handed him over. Since he didn't, they didn't. None of this had anything to do with controlling or manipulating the free decision that the citizens of Keilah were going to make. It was a decision based on knowledge of what their free decision would be. Having knowledge about what the citizens of Keilah would freely decide to do in certain circumstances made it possible for David to determine which future event would actually take place.

God's control over human decisions works like David's control over the citizens of Keilah. The difference is that God knows what would happen in every possible circumstance and has an unlimited number of ways of directing those circumstances. God's knowledge of the choices people would make in different circumstances makes it possible for him to be the controlling force in all of history. God always knows exactly what the long-term results will be for any particular action he takes. If God heals someone (or not), and if he sends a thunderstorm at a particular place and time (or not), he knows exactly what will happen in the future as a result. He can determine the course of events without resorting to controlling people's minds or making us all robots.[2] And yet, we can have confidence that all events, even evil actions, are part of God's good plan.

God's knowledge and control helps us understand how he could accomplish his purposes for Joseph. God knew what Joseph's brothers would do in a certain set of circumstances. In order to bring about the greatest good, God chose to bring about those circumstances. Joseph understood this. He knew that his brothers sinned against him. They caused him great pain. Joseph could have focused on their sin alone. But he also recognized that God was at work. He recognized the power of God to accomplish good, even in the evil acts of others.

The Bible frequently emphasizes man's wickedness and God's good, sovereign control. Consider the ultimate example: Jesus's death on the cross. This was the greatest act of evil in all of human history. Jesus was an innocent man who was convicted and sentenced to death in a sham trial. Not only was he innocent of the charges brought against him; he was the only defendant who was ever truly innocent of all wrongdoing. And Jesus was no ordinary man. He was the rightful ruler over the entire world. The crowd that demanded his death owed their lives to him. They "killed the author of life" (Acts 3:19).

Peter addressed some of the people from this same crowd in a sermon he gave less than two months after the Crucifixion. He connected Joseph's statement in Genesis 50:20 with the events surrounding Jesus's death. Peter declared, "This man was handed over to you by God's deliberate plan and foreknowledge; and you, with the help of wicked men, put him to death by nailing him to the cross" (Acts 2:23). Everything that happened to Jesus was carefully planned by God. He even spoke about it through prophets hundreds of years before it happened. Yet, according to Peter, the men involved were responsible for their evil acts.

Even though this was the greatest act of injustice in history, it was also the greatest moment for good in history. Consider that contrast for a moment. It was because of the evil done at the cross that every one of us can have our sins forgiven and know the living God. In this moment, God most clearly demonstrated "his own love for us" (Romans 5:8) If God can accomplish the greatest good from the greatest evil, there is nothing he cannot accomplish through your pain and suffering; this is the power of God!

## Does God Want Evil?

Does this mean that God delights in evil actions, gleefully bringing them about to accomplish greater things? Not at all. God "commands all people everywhere to repent" and will "judge the world with justice" (Acts 17:30–31). However, God recognizes two perspectives on evil. The short-term view is the time at which the evil is done. God hates evil from this perspective. But God also views evil with full knowledge of all that will result from the evil. He delights in this perspective because he has directed the events to accomplish his good purposes. There is nothing good in the evil itself, but there is good in its effects.[3]

Similarly, I have two kinds of feelings about lifting weights. On the one hand, I would love to have big muscles (I'm a pretty scrawny guy). On the other hand, I've never committed myself to doing the hard work of regularly lifting weights so that I can enjoy the long-term results. I have two perspectives on lifting weights. In the long-term view, I like the idea of the results that would come from regular weight training. In the short-term view, when I'm just thinking about the pain of one workout, I don't like it at all.

Now, in my case, the dislike of the short-term pain outweighs my consideration of the long-term gain. That is why I've never committed to working out. But there are many weightlifters out there who prefer the long-term benefit to the short-term pain. Their focus on the long-term results motivates them to keep working out.

God is someone who has the perfect preferences when it comes to balancing the right choice between short-term pain and long-term gain. Of course, God is dealing with greater rewards and consequences than a weight training program. Nevertheless, we can trust that God has a good purpose behind what he is doing in history and our own lives. We can trust him because he demonstrated at the cross that he can direct the greatest possible outcome in the midst of the greatest possible evil.

## Is Every Act of Evil for the Good?

At this point, you may wonder if every act is something that is under God's direction. "Sure," you're willing to admit, "God directed some of the 'big things,' like Jesus's Crucifixion, to accomplish great things. But what about when I stubbed my toe this morning? Did God direct that?" Jesus expected you to ask this question, and he answered it: "Are not two sparrows sold for a penny? Yet not one of them will fall to the ground outside your Father's care" (Matthew 10:29). According to Jesus, every pain and evil action must pass God's approval.

Paul described his confidence in God in the midst of suffering this way: "And we know that in all things God works for the good of those who love him, who have been called according to his purpose" (Romans 8:28). Paul declared that God's work in directing events, including pain and suffering, applies to all things. There is nothing too big or small that falls outside of God's work. Everything is for the good.

Now, I must clarify what Paul means by "good." Perhaps Paul was merely saying that God will bring something good, however small, out of every act of evil. The good may be nothing more than a consolation prize, but at least some good will come out of every painful event. This views God's providence like a visit to the dentist.

When I was child, I had to have some teeth pulled. It was a very painful experience. After waiting nervously while listening to other children cry, I had a big needle shoot Novocain in my sensitive gums. Then it was time to actually have the teeth pulled out of my mouth. And it wasn't over. I still had to sit uncomfortably in the chair for what seemed like an hour, with huge cotton gauzes jammed in my mouth to absorb the blood.

But there was some good that came out of it. On my way out, I got to pick out a prize from the treasure chest. Did this make it all worth it to me? Of course not! If you've ever seen the prizes that dentists give to children, you know that they are the cheapest things that could possibly be called a "prize." They couldn't cost more than a nickel each. I think I got a plastic frog that has a place in the back where you can push down on one end so that it will jump more than half an inch high. Was all the pain worth it for that? No way.

This is not what Paul means when he says "in all things God works for the good." It is not that God produces something good that partially compensates evil. Rather, the good he produces is actually greater than the evil. Paul explained, "I consider that our present sufferings are not worth comparing with the glory that will be revealed in us" (Romans 8:18). I will revisit this topic later in chapter 12, "Suffering."

## God Is Love

Recognizing God's control over events is one part of the perspective we need to sustain us through life's difficulties. However, we need to know more about God than his power over all things. We also need to know that he has good intentions for us in the way he directs events. We must know that God loves us. Specifically, I need to know that God loves me. The one who has perfect control over all events knows me and loves me.[4] The Bible has much to say to answer doubts that naturally come up about this topic.

First, the Bible tells us that God is love (1 John 4:8). The Bible also gives us a rational basis for believing that this is so. That is important because it is not immediately obvious what it means to say

God is love. Consider what God was doing before creation, before anything else existed. Do you picture God sitting in empty space, wondering to himself what he should do to pass all the time until a creation exists for him to love? Wouldn't that be strange?

Think about it; did God only begin to love when there was a creation to love? Before there was a creation, did he exist for all eternity without ever loving anything? How could anyone then say that God is love? Isn't it true that God needed something else, a creation, so that he could love? If love is something God only began to do when he created, then we could say that God has loved at times, but it would be wrong to assume that love is part of who he is.

However, there is a solution. According to the Bible, God's love is not something that began at some point in history. In other words, God has always loved. He has always loved because he has never really been alone. God has always existed in three persons, with deep love among them. Jesus expressed this in his prayer to God the Father: "Father, I want those you have given me to be with me where I am, and to see my glory, the glory you have given me because you loved me before the creation of the world" (John 17:24).

The Bible teaches that God is a triune God. God the Father, God the Son, and God the Holy Spirit have shared perfect love with each other within the Godhead for all eternity. There was no need to create in order to have something to love. God could love perfectly within the Trinity, without an external creation. Those who believe that God is absolutely one, with no distinction in persons, cannot account for how God, in his very essence, is love. However, the biblical view of God has no trouble with this problem.[5]

God did not decide to create Adam and Eve out of loneliness and a need to have someone to love. He does not need anything. He chose to create people and love them out of the overflow of love that he was already sharing within the Trinity. God then demonstrated this love for us at the cross (Romans 5:8).

Imagine that you have traveled back in time to the moment before God created Adam and Eve. Consider God's perspective at this moment. Remember that God knows everything that will happen and everything that would happen in any given situation. He knew that creating the first people and giving them freedom to choose to obey him or not would lead to sin entering the world, along with death and pain. Knowing this, God had at least three basic options.

First, he could have decided against creating beings with the choice to obey or disobey. There would be no sin, death, and pain. But there would also never be free creatures who could participate in God's love. There would either be no creatures at all or robot-like creatures that had no freedom or true personhood.

Second, God could have created people and allowed them to fall into sin with no hope of redemption. He could have left them to suffer the just consequences of their own sinful choices. "I gave them a chance," God could have reasoned. "Now they are experiencing what they deserve."

However, God had a third option. He could decide to create people he knew would disobey, while having already decided to send Jesus to die on the cross to pay for their sins and redeem them. God chose the last option based on his love. It is only the last option that would cost him greatly. Only a God who is love would choose this last option, which included a plan to love his sinful people by giving his one and only Son.

God's love for us is not merely a general love for all humanity but a personal love for you specifically. Jesus drew attention to God's love for each individual. He told a story about a man who owned a hundred sheep, and one of them wondered off. The man left the ninety-nine sheep to find the one that wandered off. The man didn't just love his sheep generally; he loved each one personally. When one wandered off, he didn't love it less; he loved it more. Jesus said that when he found it, the man was "happier about that one sheep than about the ninety-nine that did not wander off" (Matthew 18:12–14).

I know from my own experience that losing things tends to make them more valuable to me. I lost a pair of headphones once. They didn't mean that much to me—until I lost them. Once I knew they were lost, I started tearing the house apart, looking for them, neglecting my other responsibilities. Suppose I had known exactly where they were (in my office, ten miles away). Would I have bothered to drive there and get them? No, I would have decided I didn't really need them until the next day. But since I didn't know where they were, I was willing to spend hours of my time and expend lots of energy looking for them. They became more valuable in my eyes.

Jesus compared himself to the man looking for the lost sheep. He thinks of us and loves us individually, just like the man loved the lost sheep in a special way. Jesus is clearly referring to his desire to pursue you, not just a crowd. On the basis of this passage, I think it is fair to say that Jesus would have come to earth to die on the cross just for you. Even if you were the only one who needed a Savior, he would have come. Anytime you doubt the love of God, Jesus invites you to look back to the cross. No one could ever give you greater evidence of their love.

When we love someone, we often give them a physical or visible reminder. People buy flowers on Valentine's Day or Mother's Day. Couples exchange rings when they marry. They often write each other love notes. These all serve as visual declarations of love. What Jesus chose to endure on the cross for you created the ultimate visual declaration that he loves you more than any other human being ever could.

The Bible also tells us how God worked in the life of Joseph and others to demonstrate that the Lord is powerful and loving. He can and will accomplish great things through our suffering, even if we don't yet know how he will do it. Nothing about our circumstances can prevent us from a prosperous and successful life. As Paul declared, "No, in all these things we are more than conquerors through him who loved us" (Romans 8:37).

1. Kenneth Keathley, *Salvation and Sovereignty* (Nashville: B & H, 2010), 37–38. For additional biblical examples that support God having and using middle knowledge, see Jeremiah 38:17–18; Matthew 11:21–23, 26:24; John 15:22, 24, 18:36; and 1 Corinthians 2:8.
2. This is usually called God's "middle knowledge," which J. P. Moreland and William Lane Craig define as "God's knowledge of what every free creature he could create would do in every possible circumstance in which they could be placed." Craig notes that this knowledge does not determine what people will do, "but rather rests on what those choices will be." See J. P. Moreland and William Lane Craig, *Philosophical Foundations for a Christian Worldview* (Downers Grove, IL: IVP Academic, 2003), 282.
3. Jay Adams, *How to Handle Trouble* (Phillipsburg, NJ: P&R Publishing), 36.
4. Heath Lambert, *A Theology of Biblical Counseling* (Grand Rapids, MI: Zondervan, 2016), 129–30.
5. Michael Reeves, *Delighting in the Trinity* (Downers Grove, IL: InterVarsity, 2012), 19–40.

---

## ⚬ CHAPTER 6 ⚬
# PUTTING IT ALL TOGETHER

---

Not that I have already obtained all this, or have
already arrived at my goal, but I press on to take hold
of that for which Christ Jesus took hold of me.

—Philippians 3:12

The apostle Paul wrote these words in the last few years of his life.
He had already preached the Gospel throughout much of the Roman
world, started countless churches, and wrote many books of the
Bible. Even with a resume like this, Paul recognized that he was a
work in progress. He recognized that Jesus "took hold" of him for a
good goal and purpose, and he also committed himself to "press on
to take hold" of that goal.

So far, I have proposed that the Bible is the ultimate guide to
successful living. It defines the right goal of life, tells you how to get
started in pursuing that goal, and gives all the instruction you need
to keep pursuing the goal with success. I have described the major
biblical concepts that are foundational to pursuing a prosperous and
successful life. The following five steps summarize this process:

## Steps to Pursuing God's Plan for Your Life

### 1. Pursue the Right Goal.

View everything you do in life in the context of an overarching goal: glorifying God. Glorifying him includes loving him, his Word, and his will. Above all things, desire his love, a close relationship with him, and a life that draws attention to his goodness.

### 2. Trust in Jesus as the Only Hope of Reaching the Goal.

Recognize that sin has made it impossible for you to successfully pursue the right goal on your own. You have deeply broken your ability to have a close relationship with God by acting out against him and his Word. Yet you must also trust that he loves you and has provided a way for forgiveness and restoration. Place your faith in Jesus and what he did for you in his death and resurrection as the sufficient and only way of getting on the path to pursuing the goal.

### 3. Keep Changing Your Thinking.

The Joshua 1:8 promise tells us to meditate on God's law day and night. Sin that remains in our own physical bodies continuously warps our thinking when it comes to understanding who God is and how we can live in a way that is pleasing to him. You must work continuously at bringing your thinking in line with what God tells you in the Bible by studying it and meditating on it. Trust the Holy Spirit and the power of God's Word to bring about real heart changes, which will also lead to changes in your thinking.

### 4. Work on Changing Behavior.

We cannot adequately change our thinking without also changing our behavior. We cannot change our behavior without changing our thinking. The two go hand in hand. The formula for being prosperous and successful found in Joshua 1:8 is to meditate on God's law "so that you may be careful to do everything written in it." You must implement concrete action steps into your life as you work on changing your thinking. As you do so, God's Word will become effective at changing the deepest desires and affections of your heart, which direct your thoughts.

## 5. Be Prosperous and Successful.

The more you align your thinking and behavior with biblical teaching, the more you will succeed in glorifying God in your life. You will function according to the way God designed you. You can expect the accompanying benefits of joy, peace, and fulfillment in life. This is a process, and all of us have room to grow.

## Getting Specific

These five steps summarize how to become prosperous and successful generally. They do not develop action plans for specific challenges we face in life. In the following chapters, I will describe how the biblical process relates to six of the most important aspects of our lives: relationships, sex, work and money, prayer, joy, and suffering. I will show how the Bible challenges our thinking and behavior in each of these six areas and how to fit each of them into the overall goal of living for God's glory.

Before I begin to address these critical areas, I want to give an example to demonstrate how the biblical process works. Worry is a common problem to all of us. The Bible describes it as a burden, observing that it "weighs down the heart" (Proverbs 12:25). We also know from personal experience that worry can cause us to lose sleep, feel uncomfortable, and develop other health problems (which lead to further worry). Struggle with worry can even lead to panic attacks and other debilitating problems. Worry is an example of a problem we can easily identify as a hindrance to being prosperous and successful.

You may not view worry as a significant problem in life; perhaps you do. Either way, everyone has room for improvement. The good news is that the Bible tells us how to find rest from this burden. Whether you worry a little or a lot, I hope this section demonstrates how the Bible can help you be prosperous and successful with every problem in life.

## Jesus on Worry

Jesus gave significant attention to the problem of worry in the Sermon on the Mount. He began to address the topic with the command, "Therefore I tell you, do not worry about your life" (Matthew 6:25). That sounds great, right? Immediately, we recognize that this command is for our good. We have no problem seeing how our lives would be better if we could obey this perfectly.

Not all commands are like this. When Paul writes, "In humility value others above yourselves" (Philippians 2:3), it is not immediately clear that this command is for our good. It doesn't sound attractive; we sense that it might interfere with our comforts and desires. If I'm honest, when I read that command, there is part of me that wonders, "Do I really want to value others above myself?" I have no such struggle with the command against worrying. It would be wonderful if I never worried about anything again.

Distinguishing between commands I like and commands I don't like is really a reflection of a problem with my thinking. If my thinking is correct, I will understand and trust that all commands are for my good in the same way that I recognize that the command against worrying is for my good. Since God loves me and designed me to be able to enjoy life, he would never give me an instruction that doesn't contribute to an enjoyable life. The problem is not with the commands but my perception of them.

However, I am choosing to begin discussing the specifics of the biblical process of change with "Do not worry," because it is easy to see that it is a good command. It is a good first step for building trust in the Bible. I am starting with a popular command in order to build toward the more unpopular commands in subsequent chapters. However, I must note that there is a certain amount of overlap in all the commands. For example, part of the way we overcome worry is to follow the other commands, like valuing others above ourselves. I will come back to this later.

## Jesus on Overcoming Worry

The problem with the command to not worry has nothing to do with our desire to comply. The problem is a question of how. *How* do I stop worrying? No matter how much I may want to stop worrying, I cannot just say over and over in my head, "Do not worry." It won't work. If all Jesus said about the subject was, "Don't do it," we'd be in trouble. We might want to say back to Jesus, "Sure, that's a great command, but what good does it do me? I already wanted to stop worrying. Hearing you say, 'Stop it,' doesn't help me." Fortunately, Jesus didn't only say, "Stop it." He gave us the strategy we need to follow this command.

Before I explain Jesus's strategy, let me begin with a warning. I am not saying that the strategy is easy to follow. It requires hard work. But consider the alternative; continuing to worry is not easy, either. Remember, pursuing the prosperous and successful life is not always easy, but it is worth it. It would be nice if the answer to worry was that Jesus simply took away all our problems so we no longer had anything to worry about, but that is not the solution Jesus offers. He told us, "In this world you will have trouble, but take courage! I have overcome the world" (John 16:33).

What Jesus does offer is a strategy to overcome worry in the midst of problems. The first part of the strategy involves a behavioral change. Jesus referred to it in the very first word of the command not to worry: "*Therefore* I tell you, do not worry about your life" (Matthew 6:25, emphasis added). He began with "therefore," because the reason we are not to worry is based on the previous verse, where Jesus said, "Do not store up for yourselves treasures on earth ... but store up for yourselves treasures in heaven" (Matthew 6:19–20). Jesus adds, "For where your treasure is, there your heart will be also" (Matthew 6:21).

Worry is in part due to our attachment to the things of this world. We believe we will only be happy to the extent that our earthly possessions are safe. How do we break that wrong thinking? We shift our attachment to the things of heaven. We begin devoting time and resources to building the kingdom of God. We change our behavior as it relates to storing up money.

The second part of the strategy to overcome worry is to change thinking. Jesus continued with the question, "Is not life more than food, and the body more than clothes?" (Matthew 6:25). This question is a call for us to consider what life is all about. What is our goal in life? Is it really to accumulate things and safety? Then we will never feel satisfied and secure. Instead, Jesus again pointed us to focus on glorifying God as the overarching goal of life by concluding his section on worry with, "But seek first his kingdom and his righteousness" (Matthew 6:33).

Jesus gave additional thinking exercises to help overcome worry. Consider his next statement as a counseling homework assignment: "Look at the birds of the air; they do not sow or reap or store away in barns, and yet your heavenly Father feeds them" (Matthew 6:26). I take Jesus seriously here. If you want to overcome worry, set aside some time to go out and look at the birds of the air. Think about life from their perspective. Consider how silly it would be for them to worry about their provisions.

Watching the birds is important because it will help you think correctly about God. Jesus did not say to merely look at the birds, but to think about how "your heavenly Father feeds them." In chapter 5, we saw that the key to Joseph's success was the way that he thought about God. He had confidence in God's goodness and power. Joseph demonstrated that "you cannot be the same when you realize that the God who fixed the stars and planets in place directs his attention to caring for you."[1]

Furthermore, Jesus asked, "Can any one of you by worrying add a single hour to your life?" (Matthew 6:27). Of course, the answer is no. Every time you find that you are worrying, you should stop and ask yourself this question in order to remind yourself how futile it is to worry. Repeating the question regularly will help you change your thinking over time.

Finally, Jesus identified a lack of faith in the goodness and sovereignty of God as a root cause of worry. He told us that even something as fleeting as grass is beautifully clothed by God. The he asked, "If that is how God clothes the grass of the field ... will he not much more clothe you, you of little faith?" (Matthew 6:30). A lack of faith in God opens the door to worry. We must change the attitude of our hearts to reflect the truth about God as revealed in the Bible. God is a good God who cares about us and is in complete control of every situation. In addition, he knows exactly what our needs are. When our hearts are committed to this understanding of God, there is no room for worry. Yes, difficult times will come, but God is in control. He will only let us go through what is ultimately for the good (Romans 8:28).

How do we change our thoughts about God in order to increase our faith and overcome worry? One way is to meditate on God's Word day and night. Another is prayer. In the same sermon, Jesus counseled, "Ask and it will be given to you; seek and you will find; knock and the door will be opened to you" (Matthew 7:7). When you find that your faith is not sufficient enough to keep your worrying under control, study Bible verses about the goodness and power of God. Ask him to help you to grow in your confidence that what the Bible says about him is true.

In this brief passage, Jesus outlined a comprehensive strategy to overcoming worry. If you struggle with worry, you can find relief by implementing the following steps based on this one passage in the Bible. The list is an example of what I might give as homework to someone I am counseling:

## 1. Foundations

Make sure you have the right goal for life (glorify God) and have started on that journey by trusting in Jesus as Lord and Savior (see chapters 1 and 3).

## 2. Address thinking

    A. What do you really believe about God's goodness and power? What Bible passages can you study to help you grow in this area? The story of Joseph, which I discussed in chapter 5, would be a good example. Memorize a verse like Romans 8:28. Regularly meditate on what God says about himself in his Word.

B. Record in a journal what you are worrying about each time you realize you are worrying. End each entry by writing, "How does worrying about this help solve the problem?"

C. Spend at least twenty minutes during the week observing birds while considering how odd it would be for the birds to worry about their provisions, given that God is watching over them.

## 3. Address behavior

What specific ways can you begin storing up more treasure in heaven? This may include volunteering time for a ministry, giving to a charity, or developing a ministry skill like music.

## 4. Prayer

Ask God to help you grow faith in him and change your thinking about life's problems (see chapter 10, "Prayer").

## Conclusion

The list above is a beginning strategy for addressing worry that could develop over time. It is based on biblical teaching. The recommendations are similar to cognitive behavioral therapy (CBT) because they assume that changing thinking and behavior will change the emotion of worrying. They are different from CBT in that the thinking and behavioral recommendations are based on the authoritative teachings of the Bible, with the belief that these instructions come from a God who knows everything about us and wants to help us. In addition, these recommendations go beyond CBT because they address spiritual issues. In my experience, a person who is faithful in doing these assignments will see the burden of worrying decrease over time.

If you struggle greatly with worry, you may need to meet with a biblical counselor or someone in your church who can give you regular encouragement to work on this list. A biblical counselor could give additional assignments that relate to your particular problems. Is there a specific topic that you are worrying about? The Bible will address it. Perhaps you need more work on more foundational issues related to the goal of life. The Bible has endless resources for this as well.

Although the list above was created specifically to address worrying, it is not dramatically different from a list I would create for almost any other burdensome problem in life. In the following pages, I will address six key areas of life from a biblical perspective. If you are prosperous and successful in these six areas, I believe you will be well on your way to a prosperous and successful life. The Bible addresses each of these issues (and many more). In each one, the key is to have the right foundation, the right thinking, and the right behavior. All of us can and need to grow in our thinking and behavior in each area.

You will notice that there is often a certain amount of overlap in thinking and behavior for each subject. For example, I mentioned earlier that the command to "value others above yourselves" (Philippians 2:3) is not as popular as the command, "Do not worry." Yet, valuing others above yourself is an example of a thinking pattern that will help reduce worry. You cannot worry about your own problems as much when your focus shifts to the problems of others. The way we think about others is important to build strong relationships and a successful life. I will focus on what the Bible says about relationships in the next chapter.

---

1.  Lambert, *A Theology of Biblical Counseling*, 104.

# PART II
## PURSUING SUCCESS IN SIX KEY AREAS OF LIFE

---

## ‑❧ CHAPTER 7 ❧‑

# RELATIONSHIPS

---

Do not seek revenge or bear a grudge against anyone among your people, but love your neighbor as yourself. I am the Lord.

—Leviticus 19:18

One of the first stories in the Bible is about relationship problems between two brothers. Cain and Abel both brought offerings to present to God. Abel's offering was from the "fat portions from some of the firstborn of his flock," while Cain brought "some of the fruits of the soil" (Genesis 4:3–4). The words "fat portions" and "firstborn" draw attention to the quality of Abel's offering, explaining why God "looked with favor on Abel and his offering, but on Cain and his offering he did not look with favor" (Genesis 4:4–5). When Cain perceived that God was more pleased with Abel's offering, he was immediately filled with jealousy. Things went downhill from there, quickly leading to the world's first murder. The tragic story of Cain and Abel occurs right after humankind's fall into sin and highlights the devastating effects of sin on relationships.

Relationships are all around us. We are not designed to live life alone on an island. Usually, our first close relationships are with parents and siblings, and we learn right away how challenging it can be to keep a relationship running smoothly. Then come classmates, friends, other relatives, and neighbors; later, we may have a spouse and children of our own. If we have terrible relationships, we will certainly feel "weary and burdened" (Matthew 11:18) and not "prosperous and successful" (Joshua 1:8).

The Bible has so much to say about relationships. Almost every page mentions something about loving others, forgiveness, or communication. Jesus said the greatest commandment is found in Deuteronomy 6:5: "Love the LORD your God with all your heart and with all your soul and with all your mind." The highest priority in life is a relationship with God. But then Jesus added what he called the second most important command in the Bible: "Love your neighbor as yourself." Jesus continued, "All the Law and the Prophets hang on these two commandments" (Matthew 22:37–40).

According to Jesus, every command in the Bible is really an elaboration of one of these two commands. If we follow the Joshua 1:8 model to success, there are two main things we will be doing: loving God and loving people. Even these two commands are not totally separate categories. The Bible emphasizes loving others because that is the primary way to love God. Loving your neighbor as yourself is a nonnegotiable means to loving God. John wrote, "Dear friends, let us love one another, for love comes from God. Everyone who loves has been born of God and knows God" (1 John 4:7). John tells us it is impossible to know God without loving others. If we cannot even know God without loving others, it follows that we cannot love God without loving others. It is impossible to follow the greatest commandment without following the second. They are intricately tied together.

Therefore, if we want to be successful in life, we must love one another. The ultimate goal of life is to glorify God, and God has appointed loving others as a primary way we pursue that goal. As beings created in God's image, we function best when we love others the way that he loves us. That is easier said than done. Our sinful nature fills us with selfish desires that pull us away from fulfilling God's call on our lives in this area.

Cain serves as an early warning of how easily relationships can go wrong and throw us off the path of success. The Bible says that Cain "was very angry, and his face was downcast" (Genesis 4:5). God then assumed the role of Cain's counselor. He spoke to Cain, beginning by addressing his wrong thinking: "If you do what is right, will you not be accepted?" (Genesis 4:7). God reminded Cain that Abel had done nothing wrong. It was Cain's own sin that led to his anger. Next, he warned Cain that "sin is crouching at your door; it desires to have you, but you must rule over it" (Genesis 4:7).

God knew that Cain's anger was causing him to enter a downward spiral that would lead to pain and misery. Even at this point, Cain's face was downcast, revealing that his anger had become a great burden for him in life. A few verses later, the Bible records Cain's tragic failure in his battle with sin. He murdered his brother Abel, provoking God's curse on his ability to grow crops and dooming him to be a wanderer on the earth. Cain described this burden as "more than I can bear" (Genesis 4:9–13).

Cain's problems began with a lack of love for God. He didn't live with a passion to love and glorify his creator. He didn't bring the best of what he had as an offering to God the way that his brother Abel had. His lack of love for God grew out of a self-centered heart. He compounded his problems by attacking and killing his brother, also an act of selfishness. Cain's actions demonstrated how the two greatest commandments work together. The more you love God, the more you will love others. The more you love others, the deeper your relationship to God will become.

James explained the root cause of Cain's actions as well as the source of our problems with others when he wrote, "What causes fights and quarrels among you? Don't they come from your desires that battle within you? You desire but do not have, so you kill. You covet but you cannot get what you want, so you quarrel and fight" (James 4:1–2). When we fail to love others, it is because of the desires that battle within us. In order to improve our relationships, we must address problems in our thinking and our behavior.

## Thinking

We make helpful changes to our thinking about others when we meditate on the Bible. We must identify where our thinking about others is different from what the Bible says about others. For instance, when we think about others, we should recognize that they are made in the image of God. We should also recognize that Jesus Christ died to pay for their sins. God desires to bless them, forgive them, and give them eternal life. Remember that you can serve God by serving them. According to Jesus, "Whatever you did for one of the least of these brothers and sisters of mine, you did for me" (Matthew 25:40). Finally, know that you are following Jesus when you consider their interests before your own: "In humility value others above yourselves, not looking to your own interests but each of you to the interests of the others" (Philippians 2:3–4).

Let me suggest a few specific questions to help you evaluate how you are doing with biblical thinking. Ask yourself, "How many things do I think about doing for myself each morning before I ask the question, 'How can I be a blessing to others today?'" When you recognize that you have mistreated someone, ask yourself, "How am I being like Cain? What desires have led to negative attitudes or actions toward this person?" If you regularly ask yourself questions like these, the way you think about others will begin to change.

## Behavior

Jesus addressed behavior with his shocking parable of the Good Samaritan in Luke 10. A Jewish expert of the law was discussing the command "Love your neighbor as yourself" with Jesus and wanted clarification on an important point. He asked Jesus, "And who is my neighbor?" Jesus answered by telling a story about a man who was beaten and left half-dead on the side of the road. Two Jewish religious leaders, a priest and a Levite, saw him but did nothing for him as they passed by. Then a Samaritan, a rival of the Jews, saw him. Unlike the others, he did everything he could do to help the man. He bandaged the man's wounds and brought him to town on his own donkey. He even left money to cover his medical expenses and came back later to check on him.

Jesus ended the story with the piercing question, "Which of these three do you think was a neighbor to the man who fell in the hands of the robbers?" (Luke 10:29). When the expert of the law gave the obvious answer, "The one who had mercy on him," Jesus responded, "Go and do likewise." His concluding words sound a lot like a counseling homework assignment to me. Jesus was saying that it's not just enough to agree that loving others is important. You must go and do it. Jesus's counsel to the man was to go and find someone in need who was not expecting help and give sacrificially.

What about us? Rather than thinking of this as a vague teaching, what if we actually did it? It's easy to nod our heads in agreement with the parable of the Good Samaritan and think, *That's right, Jesus. We need to love everyone like the Good Samaritan.* It's another thing altogether to get specific. Find someone *this week* who needs help and is not expecting it from you and give of yourself to meet their needs. Give of your time, or finances, or both. Go and do likewise. Not theoretically, or one day, but now.

If you are like most people, you may wonder, "That sounds nice, but what's in it for me?" First, behavior and thinking work together. Implementing specific action steps to do things for others is critical to changing how you think about others. As your thinking changes, your behavior will get easier to change and will keep changing. You will enjoy what you are doing. You will function more and more the way God designed you. In short, you will become prosperous and successful. "If you spend yourselves in behalf of the hungry and satisfy the needs of the oppressed, then your light will rise in the darkness, and your night will become like the noonday" (Isaiah 58:10).

## Forgiveness

Forgiving others is essential to loving them. Just as I cannot love God without loving others, I cannot love others without regularly forgiving them. Therefore, a commitment to forgiving others is a necessary part of being prosperous and successful.

The Bible frequently emphasizes the importance of forgiveness. Jesus taught us to pray "forgive us our debts, as we also have forgiven our debtors" (Matthew 6:12). That almost sounds as if God will not forgive us if we do not forgive others. In fact, Jesus clarified that was indeed his intended meaning. He went on to state plainly, "If you do not forgive others their sins, your Father will not forgive your sins" (Matthew 6:15). Given this statement, it is not possible to overestimate the importance of forgiveness in the Christian life.

At another time, Jesus stated, "If your brother or sister sins against you, rebuke them; and if they repent, forgive them. Even if they sin against you seven times in a day and seven times come back to you saying 'I repent,' you must forgive them" (Luke 17:3–4). If people repent of the wrong they have done to you, you are required to forgive them. If they don't repent, you are to "rebuke them" with the goal of getting them to acknowledge the wrong they have done and repent so that you can forgive.

You are to forgive in this way without limit. In Luke, Jesus said "seven times in a day." Imagine this happening in real life. You come home from a shopping trip on Saturday morning and find that the neighbor has taken your lawnmower out of your shed and is using it to cut his grass. You told him the day before that you were planning on mowing your lawn today. Now you're not sure you will have enough gas to get the job done. When he sees you, he realizes what he has done and brings the lawnmower back. "I'm sorry," he tells you. "I forgot that you needed it today, and besides, I shouldn't ever take something of yours without your permission." You are then required to forgive him.

Suppose you go inside for a few minutes but suddenly hear the lawnmower running again at your neighbor's house. "I'm sorry again," he says after you go outside to get his attention. He starts bringing the lawnmower back while saying, "It's just that I was so close to finishing, and I wanted to get it done. I shouldn't have done it without asking."

Again, you are required to forgive him.

But later, while you're mowing your lawn, you see him sneaking out of your yard with your weed eater in his hands! *What's with this guy?* you ask yourself. Again, he apologizes, and again, you forgive him. Guess what? Your neighbor has sinned against you three times in a day. Imagine if this kept going on until that evening, with your neighbor sinning against you and then repenting seven times. On one occasion, Jesus even commented that we should forgive "not seven times, but seventy-seven times"[1] (Matthew 18:22). There's no way to call this anything other than radical forgiveness.

Forgiveness is sort of like the command to not worry. We like the concept. We recognize that it would be good for us to not worry, and we also recognize that it would be good for us to radically forgive others. Holding on to anger may cause loss of sleep, stress, and consequences to our health. Besides, it doesn't feel good. But the obvious question is, how? I may want to be a forgiving person, but how do I do it?

Let's start with the issue of defining forgiveness. What exactly is it that you are doing when you forgive someone? Jesus addressed both the definition of forgiveness and how to do it in a jarring parable about an unmerciful servant. The servant owed his master "ten thousand bags of gold" (Matthew 18:24). A typical worker at this time would need 193,000 years to earn that much money.[2] He had no way to repay the debt. The master had every legal right to throw him into prison and sell his wife and children into slavery. The servant begged for more time. His fate was in the master's hands.

The master decided to show the debtor mercy. He could have done this by granting more time for payment. Perhaps he could also reduce the debt to give the servant a better chance of paying it back. But that is not what the master decided to do. Instead, he completely canceled the debt. The books were cleared. After the meeting, the servant didn't owe the master a single penny.

Jesus uses this story as an illustration for forgiveness. Forgiveness is primarily the cancelling of a debt. When someone sins against you, they owe you. You have certain rights, including the right to be angry with them. When you forgive them, you are canceling their debt. You are laying down your right to be angry.

Laying down your right to be angry can really be broken down into four specific promises.[3] For example, the first promise is, "I will not use this against you." Imagine a husband and wife arguing. The wife starts with a simple expression of frustration: "Why didn't you take out the trash this morning?" Annoyed, the husband seeks to justify himself by pointing out that his wife also forgets her responsibilities at times: "You're one to talk; you didn't remember to pay the electric bill on time last month." Now, it's on! The husband and wife go back and forth like a tennis match, responding to each insult by bringing up another mistake from their spouse's past. They steadily work backward in time, creating a detailed history lesson of each other's mistakes.

Finally, the husband believes he has the winning shot. "Oh yeah?" he begins, right after she cried out that he didn't get her anything for their second anniversary fourteen years earlier. He exclaims, "I'll end this right now. Don't you remember that the month before we got engaged, you ..." But then he suddenly stops. "Oh, wait, I can't bring that one up," he says. "I forgave you for that."

By forgiving her, the husband gave up his right to use it against her. He cancelled her debt. She gets to "win" the argument because he has given her the gift of forgiveness. I put *win* in quotation marks because nobody ever really wins an argument like this. But when a husband and wife learn to extend radical forgiveness to each other, they both win. If they had forgiven each other for each transgression, neither one of them would have had anything to bring up in the argument, other than the immediate issue at hand; all previous debts would have been cancelled.

Forgiveness is hard because it gives something of great value to another person without the promise of anything in return, just like the master who forgave his servant's great debt. Three other promises are also implied in forgiveness: "I will not talk to others about this incident," "I will not dwell on this incident," and "I will not let this incident continue to harm our relationship." Forgiveness implies a commitment to avoid these three acts because doing any of them would communicate that there is still a debt to be paid in the offended person's mind.

When you are angry, you tell others about what someone has done because you want to embarrass them or harm their reputation. You dwell on the matter and give someone the cold shoulder. Previously, when you passed them in the hallway at work, you'd say, "Hey, how are you?" Now you avoid them. Forgiveness, however, does away with all that. Forgiveness means the anger and retribution cease. When you forgive someone who has sinned against you, you give something to the person who hurt you, sometimes at great expense to yourself.

## How to Forgive

Jesus's parable about forgiveness does not end with the master cancelling his servant's great debt. Jesus goes on to tell us that the servant left that liberating meeting with his master and found another servant who owed him "a hundred silver coins," a sum of money that would take an average worker about three to four months to earn (Matthew 18:28). It was not a minuscule amount, but it was hundreds of thousands of times less than the "ten thousand bags of gold" the servant had owed his master. What would this forgiven servant now do with a man who owed him something? Jesus reports that "he grabbed him and began to choke him. 'Pay back what you owe me!' he demanded." After the man begged for more time, the servant had him thrown into prison (Matthew 18:28–29).

Of course, when the other servants heard what happened, they were horrified. Jesus gave this parable to teach us how we can forgive. It starts with our perspective and what we really believe about our own sin and what God has done for us. Forgiving is hard, just like it would be hard to cancel a debt of a hundred silver coins. But what should have given the servant the ability to do it is the recognition that he had just been forgiven a much greater debt. Everyone listening to Jesus's story recognized that it was unreasonable to have such a large debt forgiven and not extend a little mercy to someone who owed a much smaller amount.

The servant may have been angry that he was not getting his money back in a timely fashion. It may have been very hard to let go of the possibility of ever getting that money back. It would have cost him a lot to say, "Don't worry about paying me back. I am cancelling your debt." However, he could have gathered the strength to do just that by thinking about the money differently. Instead of thinking of it as a personal financial loss, he could have thought about it as coming out of the large sum he had just been forgiven earlier in the day. "I may lose a lot of money by canceling this man's debt," the servant could reason to himself, "but seeing how much I was just forgiven, this is still a really great day for me. I'll just consider that I am giving to this man a small portion of what my master just gave me."

That is how God calls on us to think about the debts that others owe us. Jesus states in the Lord's Prayer, "forgive us our debts, as we also have forgiven our debtors" (Matthew 6:12). When it is hard for us to forgive, we must renew our focus on God's forgiveness of us. We can tell ourselves, "With all that God has forgiven me, I should easily be able to forgive this person. I'll just consider that I am giving a small portion of what God gave me."

Perhaps you think that God hasn't forgiven you that much. "I've never done anything as awful as what that evil monster did to me," you may claim. However, keep in mind that your sin is against a holy and perfectly loving God, who gave you life and created everything you have. The person who sinned against you is sinning against a fellow sinful creature. Your sin against God is greater than you may realize. When you have a biblical perspective on your behavior, you recognize that when you placed your faith in Christ, God forgave you far more than you could ever hope to forgive others in a lifetime.

If we really believe that God has forgiven us such a great debt, we will have no problem forgiving. It's all coming out of the account that God gave to us. We can go out and gladly dispense forgiveness to others, being reminded each time of the freedom from sin we have in Christ.

## The Tongue

I can't conclude a chapter on relationships without saying something about communication. The way we use our tongue will likely be the most significant factor in the quality of our relationships. The Bible warns that misuse of the tongue is a common way that a person's life is thrown off the prosperous and successful path. James writes that the tongue is "a fire, a world of evil among the parts of the body. It corrupts the whole body, sets the whole course of one's life on fire" (James 3:6).

While the Bible says many things about communication, there are three areas worthy of special attention. Each of these principles is related to the command, "Love your neighbor as yourself."

## 1. Listen to others more than you speak.

We all want to get our point of view across and have others understand our thoughts and feelings. So we should serve others by listening to them the way we want others to listen to us. "Everyone should be quick to listen, slow to speak, and slow to become angry" (James 1:19).

## 2. Tell the truth.

"Therefore each of you must put off falsehood and speak truthfully to your neighbor" (Ephesians 4:25). In my opinion, there are circumstances where other concerns outweigh the command to tell the truth. If you were hiding Jews in your house during World War II, and a Nazi asked if you were hiding any Jews, it would be appropriate to lie to save their lives and your own. The Bible gives examples of similar circumstances and appropriate deceitful behavior (see Exodus 2:18–19 and Joshua 2:3–4). Jesus spoke about "more important matters of the law" (Matthew 23:23), meaning that sometimes, one law takes precedence over another.

However, we can always think of some justification for lying, and in reality, many of us will never face a situation as extreme as the World War II example. We should speak truthfully to others the way we want them to speak truthfully to us. That not only means no lying but also not deceiving others by omitting key information in our answers.

## 3. Use words that build others up.

"Do not let any unwholesome talk come out of your mouths, but only what is helpful for building others up according to their needs, that it may benefit those who listen" (Ephesians 4:29). Imagine that every word you said was recorded in a book and published. Somewhere, there was a library with twelve volumes for every year of your life, one for each month of each year. A thick volume of hundreds and hundreds of pages recorded every word you spoke this month as well. Shelf after shelf in this library contained books from previous months. It is simply staggering to think how many words even an introvert says in a lifetime.

As you picture these shelves of books full of your words, try to think about what you have accomplished with those words. Have your words been a benefit to those who heard them? What portion of your words was intentionally chosen to encourage, comfort, and help others? How many of your words criticized, put down, or were used to fulfill self-centered desires? On a more practical level, it might help to spend a day or two keeping track on a tally sheet. Put a mark down in a "build others up" column when you use your words to encourage others and a mark in the "unwholesome talk" column when you use words that are not the ones you would want someone to use with you. At the end of the day, look at your results. Remember, the command is to "not let any unwholesome talk come out of your mouths."

These commands are not intended to add a burden to life but to help you evaluate if you are doing what you need to do to be prosperous and successful. If the goal of life is to glorify God, and one of the key ways we do that is to love others, and one of the key ways we do that is with the use of our tongue, then we need an honest evaluation of how we are doing. The tongue can quickly "set the whole course of one's life on fire" or can be an effective tool for becoming prosperous and successful. Have a God-honoring vision for the use of the tongue in your life.

---

1.  Or seventy times seven.
2.  David L. Turner, "Matthew," in *Baker Exegetical Commentary on the New Testament* (Grand Rapids, MI: Baker, 2008), 450.
3.  Ken Sande, *The Peacemaker* (Grand Rapids, MI: Baker, 2004), 202.

# CHAPTER 8

# SEX

How delightful is your love, my sister, my bride! How much more pleasing is your love than wine, and the fragrance of your perfume more than any spice!

—Song of Solomon 4:1

Okay, admit it. You skipped ahead quite a ways to get to this chapter, right? I'm not surprised. You are probably wondering, "Is there really a way to pursue God's plan for my life through, of all things, sex?" The Bible tells us everything we need to know so we can have a prosperous and successful life. So, yes, that includes sex. However, I mean more than simply the physical act of sex, although that is obviously part of it. I am including everything from the purpose of sex to those details about who you can have sex with and when. The Bible has a surprisingly vast amount to say about sex, which indicates that it is an important part of God's plan for us.

Samson is an obvious biblical example of the important role sex has in pursuing success in life. He is known as the Bible's strong man, almost like a superhero. Typically, he is portrayed as a large and muscular man, although that probably wasn't the case. It's true that he performed incredible feats of strength, but the Bible indicates that he did great things through the power of the Spirit of the Lord. In other words, it's unlikely that he would impress us with his bulging muscles if he were around today. There were no bodybuilders back then. The message is not that he could kill lots of people because he worked out so much, but that God gave him supernatural strength at different moments in his life.

But what Samson is best known for is his destructive relationship with a woman named Delilah. The Bible tells us that "he fell in love with" her, and Samson's enemies saw this as a weakness they could exploit (Judges 16:4–5). Unknown to Samson, Delilah was seeking out a large pile of reward money when she asked Samson, "Tell me the secret of your great strength and how you can be tied up and subdued" (Judges 16:6). Samson seemed to play around with her, telling her an obvious lie about being tied with seven fresh bowstrings. Later on, he awoke and found himself tied with seven fresh bowstrings and a group of Philistine men attacking him. God gave him the strength he needed to escape the attack, but he now knew that Delilah was out to get him.

Now, you would think that after Delilah tried to have Samson killed, he would be angry with her, end the relationship, and move out. Instead, the biblical account says that Delilah was actually angry with Samson. She whined, "You have made a fool of me; you lied to me. Come now, tell me how you can be tied" (Judges 16:10). Samson stayed with Delilah. He kept telling her stories about how she could get him captured and probably killed, and she kept trying to do it. This is a classic story of an abusive relationship. One of Delilah's arguments was, "How can you say, 'I love you,' when you won't confide in me?" (Judges 16:15). Of course, as readers of the story, we are wondering, "Why doesn't Samson ask her how she can say 'I love you,' when she repeatedly tries to get him killed?"

Perhaps you think this story is unrealistic. Nobody could be as stupid as Samson. No one would stay in a sexual relationship that was so obviously destructive to their well-being.

You're kidding, right? We see it happen all the time. Whether it's a woman who keeps coming back to her boyfriend after he's beaten her for the fifth time, or the politician who resigned in disgrace because he can't stop sexting to underage girls, people are constantly engaging in self-destructive sexual relationships. In fact, all sexual relationships that fall outside of God's purpose for sex are destructive. The story about Samson is one place where the Bible helps us to see that we can trust biblical teachings about sex more than our own judgment or our culture's views.

We may wonder how Samson could be trapped by a woman like Delilah. But Samson's problems didn't begin with her. She was the last in a long line of sexual choices that ignored biblical teaching and sent Samson's life in a downward spiral. It began when a young Samson approached his parents and said, "I have seen a Philistine woman in Timnah; now get her for me as my wife" (Judges 14:2).

The biblical account draws attention to the foolishness of young Samson's choice for a wife in several ways. He based his decision to marry on lust. He decided to marry her because he saw her, not because he knew her and had a good basis for thinking she was right for him. He didn't even know how she felt; he simply barked, "Get her for me." He also ignored the wisdom of his parents, who replied, "Isn't there an acceptable woman among your relatives or among all our people? Must you go to the uncircumcised Philistines to get a wife?" (Judges 14:3).

Indeed, Samson's parents identified the main problem with the woman from Timnah. God had appointed Samson to deliver the Israelites from the oppression of the Philistines. He had warned all the Israelites not to marry those who worshiped foreign gods because they would lead them away from the worship of the true God. How much more should the one who is called to deliver the Israelites from the Philistines stay away from a Philistine woman? But Samson did not listen. The values that guided his decision making were not, "What will help me glorify God with my life?" But rather, "What will satisfy my lusty appetites?"

The rest of Judges 14 recounts Samson's disastrous marriage. He displayed foolishness not only in who he chose to marry, but how he conducted himself with the other Philistines who made up the wedding party. During the weeklong wedding celebration, one thing led to another, culminating in his bride betraying him. Samson went on a murderous rampage to make good on a bet he lost with his own groomsmen. His wife was given to another man, and when Samson sought revenge against the Philistines for this, they burned down his wife's house, killing her and her father.

Samson was never the same. Later, he spent the night with a Philistine prostitute (Judges 16:1). Apparently, he was trying to ease the pain of losing his first love by pursuing other Philistine women. Many years later, he fell in love with the Philistine woman Delilah. I don't think Samson was stupid to stay with Delilah. I think he just didn't care anymore. His actions fit the profile of someone who is severely depressed. He knew she was trying to kill him, but he didn't know if he really wanted to go on living, anyway.

Samson could have avoided the problems he faced if he had followed God's instruction throughout his life. First, he should have made glorifying God his ultimate goal. Second, he should have followed the specific instructions about what to do and not do as he pursued the goal with his sexuality. Although it would have been difficult to exercise restraint and wait for the right Israelite woman to come along for him to marry, Samson could have saved himself years of pain. Remember, following God's way may be hard at first, but in the long run, it will be worth it.

God wants to steer us in the right direction and warn us about the many dangers that sexuality poses. He designed us for a purpose, including our sexuality. In the opening chapter, the Bible tells us that God made humankind "male and female." Then the first thing God told them was, "Be fruitful and increase in number" (Genesis 1:27–28). When God designed us, sexuality was not an afterthought; he made it a central part of who we are. God knows exactly what is best for us and how our sexuality is designed to help us pursue the goal of life. The trouble is that many biblical teachings on sex sound outdated and unreasonable to us.

Sooner or later, we all say, "I want this, even though the Bible says …" Like Samson, our desires seem right in our own minds, even if we recognize that the Joshua 1:8 promise is for those who "carefully do everything written." So this is where the rubber meets the road. Are we really going to trust Jesus that it will be better for us if we deny our desires and pursue God's glory instead, even when it comes to sex? I mean, it sounds noble and adventurous to read about taking up one's cross and following Jesus, but it's different when the context is a specific question like, "Am I really not supposed to sleep with my girlfriend?"

More than any other topic, when it comes to sex, we feel there must be some sort of mistake in our understanding about God's teaching. "God wouldn't mind if I bend the rules a little bit for this," we foolishly tell ourselves. Like Samson, we have to make the choice: "Will I trust my way or God's way?"

## God's Way

In the second chapter in the Bible, God tells us that there was a time when there was only one man on earth. There were animals with him, but no other people. God said, "It is not good for the man to be alone. I will make a helper suitable to him" (Genesis 2:18). After God made the first woman, the man was impressed because she was "bone of my bones and flesh of my flesh." The Bible concludes, "That is why a man leaves his father and mother and is united to his wife, and they become one flesh (Genesis 2:23–24).

Jesus quoted from these passages in Genesis 1 and 2 to respond to a question about divorce. He drew attention to the fact that "the Creator 'made them male and female.'" Then he quoted Genesis 2:24 about a father and mother becoming one flesh. Finally, he added his own comment: "Therefore what God has joined together, let no one separate" (Matthew 19:4–6). He insisted that although there were provisions in the Old Testament for divorce, they were only in place because of the necessity of managing sinful people. Regulations on divorce in no way validated divorce as an acceptable practice. Jesus concluded by stating, "I tell you that anyone who divorces his wife, except for sexual immorality, and marries another woman commits adultery" (Matthew 19:9).

Examining the way Jesus referred to Genesis 1 and 2 and other texts leads to several inescapable conclusions about God's plan for sexuality:

1.  God designed us to be either male or female (Genesis 2:18, 24).
2.  God designed men and women so they can have a special "one flesh" relationship with each other, which includes a sexual relationship (Genesis 2:24).
3.  A sexual relationship is designed to be in the context of a lifelong marriage relationship between one man and one woman (Matthew 19:6).
4.  Adultery occurs whenever a person in this special one-flesh relationship joins with another person, even if the person is legally divorced. In my view, it is not necessary to conclude that when a divorce occurs, both partners are committing adultery if they remarry, but at least one is (Matthew 19:6–9).[1]
5.  The marriage commitment is so important that even lusting after a person who is not your spouse is a type of adultery that occurs in the heart (Matthew 5:28).
6.  People who are pursuing God's plan for their lives are not free to marry anyone they choose. You should marry only someone who will be a partner with you in your pursuit of glorifying God with your life. A marriage relationship is intended to be so close that it will be impossible for you to pursue opposite goals in life and have the right kind of marriage. God warned the Israelites not to marry people who do not worship the same God (see, for example, Deuteronomy 7:3–4 and 2 Corinthians 6:14). Samson illustrates the danger of this. There are also a number of restrictions on marrying close relatives listed in Leviticus 18.

## Aren't There Other Interpretations?

I know that our culture fiercely opposes the points listed above. There is pressure to reinterpret the Bible to conform to our culture's understanding of sex. People often argue that you can make very different sexual choices and still follow the Bible. However, when you read the fine print of their arguments, every case made for greater sexual leniency is based on the idea that the Bible is mistaken or is not really an authoritative word from God.[2] I believe they represent the voice of the serpent all the way back in Genesis 3, asking, "Did God really say?" However, if we read the Scriptures, believing they are the authoritative Word of God, and if we can trust them to tell us what is best for us, then I truly believe we will not have any significant disagreements with the points above. However, I will address some of the most common questions that come up below:

## Does It Really Matter if We Have Sex before Marriage?

Since sex is designed as a special part of the one-flesh marriage covenant, it should not occur outside of that context. The Bible confirms this interpretation in several places. First, consider Paul's warning against prostitution: "Do you not know that he who unites himself with a prostitute is one with her in body? For it is said, 'The two will become one flesh'" (1 Corinthians 6:16). Paul argues that even in prostitution, where there is no commitment to one another whatsoever, two people join and enter a one-flesh relationship. Therefore, sex is not merely a physical act. Human beings are both physical and spiritual. God made people male and female, with spirits that in some mysterious way are joined together through sex. This goes beyond the physical act. You should only become one flesh with someone with whom you are in a lifelong covenant relationship.

That same assumption is at work in Exodus 22:16–17: "If a man seduces a virgin who is not pledged to be married and sleeps with her, he must pay the bride-price, and she shall be his wife. If her father absolutely refuses to give her to him, he must still pay the bride-price for virgins." Although the law provided a way out of marriage when premarital sex occurred, the act of sex was viewed almost like a marriage commitment itself. The idea was that if you are really close enough to someone to begin a sexual relationship with them, then you must also be ready for a marriage commitment. The two go together. If you think, *But we're just not quite ready for a marriage relationship yet*, then you should also conclude that you're not quite ready for a sexual relationship, either.

## Since Divorce Is Bad, Isn't It a Good Idea to Live Together before You Get Married?

The Bible warns against any sexual relationship outside of marriage. In my opinion, it is impossible to live with a romantic partner and not have a sexual relationship; it just doesn't happen. So living together violates biblical teaching. Even if you were somehow able to live together and avoid sex, living together in and of itself is something that married couples do in the context of a lifelong commitment to each other. There is no biblical category for "sort of" married.

Today, our culture views cohabitation as something as normal as holding hands. However, as recently as 1970, it was illegal in every state for an unmarried man and woman to live together.[3] So in the recent past, our culture recognized that there are inherent dangers with cohabitation.

In the years since then, statistics confirm that living together is a bad idea. First, the chances for divorce go up by 50 percent when couples live together before marriage. Second, only half of cohabitating couples actually marry, even though most say they intend to marry.[4] This often leads to children born to a single mother, great heartache, and problems that carry into future relationships. You may think you have a good motive for living together before marriage, but neither the Bible nor common experience support it.

## What about All the Polygamy in the Bible?

Yes, the Bible records many instances of polygamy, but this does not mean that God approved of the practice. Other than Jesus, the Bible portrays all the heroes of the faith as having serious flaws and missteps. David committed murder and adultery, Noah got drunk, Abraham let another man take his wife because he was afraid of him.

And yes, Solomon and many others had multiple wives. But Jesus said the biblical standard for marriage is found in the beginning, where God pronounced the vision for marriage as a lifetime relationship between one man and one woman.

## Does the Bible Really Condemn Same-Sex Relationships?

Leviticus 18:22 often comes up in this debate: "Do not have sexual relations with a man as one does with a woman; that is detestable." Supporters of same-sex relationships often respond by calling this one of the "clobber" verses. They mean that people use the verse as an excuse to bash gay people. After all, people who quote Leviticus 18:22 don't follow all the other strange laws in Leviticus, so why do they choose to follow this particular verse?

First, I think that supporters of same-sex relationships are right that it is possible to misuse Leviticus 18:22. A person needs a valid reason for appealing to this verse when arguing against same-sex relationships, while ignoring many other commands in Leviticus. In addition, no command in the Bible should be used as a club or excuse to sit in judgment of others. God has given commandments to guide us to true prosperity and success, not as weapons of condemnation to fight each other with. Sadly, the commandments are often not used the right way.

However, even when the commandments are used the right way, they do indicate that same-sex marriage relationships are not compatible with God's design for sexuality. This includes the Leviticus 18:22 command. Leviticus does contain many laws that are uniquely suited for the Jewish people and their special national calling. However, the sexual prohibitions listed in Leviticus 18 do not fall into that category. There is a valid reason for following the prohibitions in this chapter while not necessarily following other laws in Leviticus. The chapter specifically tells us that the list of sexual commands applies to all nations, not just Israel. "Do not defile yourselves in any of these ways, because this is how the nations that I am going to drive out before you became defiled" (Leviticus

18:24). Context lets us know that the entire list of sexual sins found in Leviticus 18 applies to everyone.

Of course, Genesis 1 and 2 already spelled out God's purpose for creating people male and female for a sexual, covenant relationship. Leviticus 18:22 removes any doubt about whether same-sex relationships can somehow fit into that vision; they can't. Jesus also supported Old Testament teaching on the topic (Matthew 5:17–19) and specifically endorsed marriage being limited to one man and one woman (Matthew 19:4-6).

One common excuse for pursuing a same-sex relationship is, "God made me this way." However, the Bible clearly tells us that none of us are the way God designed us to be. Ever since Adam and Eve sinned in the garden of Eden, all of us have become corrupted by sin. If you struggle with same-sex attraction, it does not mean God designed you that way or approves of you acting out on that desire. Nor does it mean that you will be prosperous and successful if you embrace what God calls sinful as part of your identity. The possibility of a fulfilling life truly exists in Christ and in following his commands, even for those who struggle with same-sex attraction.[5]

Another excuse is summarized by the slogan "Love wins." This apparently means that God wants us to embrace our differences and love one another. Therefore, we should celebrate those who choose same-sex relationships. Why should we have any problem with two people loving each other? However, this is an inadequate understanding of love. The Bible never prohibits two people loving each other. But it does prohibit two people of the same gender from having sex with each other. Sex is not the same as love. If you love someone, you want what is best for them. The Bible gives us God's guidelines for what is best for us, and that does not allow for same-sex relationships. No one loved others as much as Jesus did, and Jesus taught against same-sex relationships. He is the ultimate model of love.

## Is It Okay to Do Anything with Someone as Long as We Don't Have Sexual Intercourse?

If you mean, "As long as we don't do anything that could result in a pregnancy," then no. There are clear sexual acts that are prohibited even if you haven't technically had sexual intercourse. Perhaps you are thinking more along the lines of romantic kissing or touching that doesn't involve removing clothing or an overt sexual act. The Bible doesn't give a rigid guideline for these things. However, Paul does warn, "Flee from sexual immorality. All other sins a person commits are outside the body, but whoever sins sexually, sins against their own body" (1 Corinthians 6:18). We are not simply to avoid sexual immorality; we are to flee from it. A mind-set of "Let's see how far we can get without going all the way," is incredibly dangerous. Sex is very powerful, and countless people can testify that they ended up having sex with someone they never intended to because they just got carried away. I always recommend conservative standards that will help you keep you stay within God's boundaries.

## Is There Hope for Me?

I assume most readers of this chapter are wondering, "But I've already made a mistake (or many mistakes); what now?" That's the beauty of the Gospel. "But God demonstrates his own love for us in this: While we were still sinners, Christ died for us" (Romans 5:8). God does not start loving you once you've got everything together. He has always loved you. He has provided what you need to have complete forgiveness. God's teaching about sex is not there to condemn you but rather to tell you what's best for you. When we violate God's instruction, we may face painful consequences. But God can forgive your past and use you in powerful ways. The question that matters is, what will you do now?

Samson failed to follow God's teaching many times in his life. As a consequence, he was consumed by anger, disappointment, bitterness, and depression. However, there are two important things to remember about him. First, God used Samson to accomplish his purposes, even in the midst of his sin. God empowered a sinful Samson because he "was seeking an occasion to confront the Philistines" (Judges 14:4). Although it will always go better for you when you obey God, you can find comfort knowing that God can even use your sinful choices to accomplish his good purposes.

Second, Samson always had the chance to start going in the right direction again. That's called repentance. After he was captured and blinded, he was finally humble enough to see how wrong he had been to disregard God's law. He humbly prayed for help from God, who strengthened him once more. Samson died as he pushed over the pillars that held up the roof to the temple where the Philistines gathered. Although he only lived a few more moments after turning to God, I believe he felt a peace from God at that time that he had never known before. Whatever the sexual sin is in your life, you can find forgiveness and the power to change direction from this point forward.

## What Good Is Sex?

God commissioned the first people to "be fruitful and increase in number" (Genesis 1:28), designating procreation as a purpose for sex. But having children is certainly not the only purpose for sex. Proverbs 5:18–20 speaks about enjoying your spouse sexually with no reference to procreation. 1 Corinthians 7 also talks about couples needing to be with each other sexually on a regular basis in order to maintain a healthy relationship. Sex is a physical act that communicates and solidifies a spiritual union between two people. In some way, it is an important part of how two become "one flesh."

The creation account and Genesis 1 also records that God made humankind "male and female," immediately after stating that they were made in his image. The sexual relationship in a marriage helps us understand something about the love of God within the Trinity and the kind of love he extends to us. Jesus prayed "that all of them may be one, Father, just as you are in me and I am in you. May they also be in us" (John 17:21). Sex helps us experience intimacy in a way that develops our understanding of God's unity and desire for unity between himself and the church. Paul saw parallels between a husband and wife and the relationship between Jesus and the church (Ephesians 5:25). Human sexuality is a mysterious gift that increases our capacity to understand God's love.

Although not the only purpose, sex also enables people to be involved in the process of bringing children into the world. There is no biblical command to seek marriage and children, and some people can pursue God's plan and remain single throughout their lives, or may find that they cannot have children. However, many others find great blessing from God through marriage and children. When Eve gave birth to her first son, she exclaimed, "With the help of the LORD I have brought forth a man" (Genesis 4:1). Having children is one example of the power of sex to change the direction of our life in a positive way.

If we are pursuing God's goal for our lives, we need to recognize that sex is a key area that can drive us off the right path quickly and cause long-lasting damage. On the other hand, sex can be a significant part of how we pursue our ultimate goal of glorifying God. As in every area of life, being successful in the area of sex will mean embracing God's vision for it. God has designed sex to be a joyful part of our experience living for his glory.

---

1.  That is the reason for Jesus saying "except for sexual immorality" (Matthew 19:9). If adultery has already occurred, then the divorce cannot be the cause of adultery. Every divorce and remarriage means that adultery has occurred, but that does not mean that both parties are guilty of the adultery.
2.  See, for example, Matthew Vines, *God and the Gay Christian: The Biblical Case in Support of Same-Sex Relationships* (New York: Convergent, 2014).
3.  David Gudgel, *Before You Live Together* (Ventura, CA: Regal, 2003), 21.
4.  Ibid., 41–47.
5.  See David Bennett, *A War of Loves* (Grand Rapids, MI: Zondervan, 2018).

# CHAPTER 9

# WORK AND MONEY

Whatever you do, work at it with all your heart, as
working for the Lord, not for human masters.

—Colossians 3:23

God wants you to be prosperous and successful in life, and that
includes your job and finances. Most people spend at least fifty hours
a week at work when including breaks and commute time. That is
nearly half of all waking hours. Therefore, what you do in that time
makes up a significant part of what you will do in life. Naturally, it
is an important component of a successful life.

In addition, most workers also have a strong drive to earn more
money; they may even define success in financial terms. Almost
everyone recognizes an important role for finances when thinking
about the future. Therefore, it should be no surprise that God has a
lot to say about work and money. Among many other things, God
actually includes an accurate guide to getting rich fast.

## Getting Rich Fast

Yes, the Bible really does give specific principles that millions of
people have used to get rich fast, and you don't even have to work
hard! The book of Proverbs explains the wisdom of God's law in

very practical ways. It addresses the topic of money more often than any other book in the Bible. It actually gives three proven methods for accumulating lots of wealth. Are you ready? According to Proverbs, three get-rich-quick strategies are lying, injustice, and robbery.

Of course, the author of Proverbs also strongly warns against these things. For example, in the opening chapter, he describes a group of thieves who invite a young man to join them in killing someone in order to take his possessions. They promise the young man that they will "get all sorts of valuable things and fill our houses with plunder." However, Proverbs tells us that in reality, they "lie in wait for their own blood" and "all who go after ill-gotten gain" do not come out ahead (Proverbs 1:13, 18–19). You can get rich this way, but it isn't worth it.

Later, Proverbs 21:6 says, "A fortune made by a lying tongue is a fleeting vapor and a deadly snare." Notice that the verse affirms that you can make a fortune through lying, but it also warns that it will not last and that it brings dangers that are not worth it. Or, "Better a little with righteousness than much gain with injustice" (Proverbs 16:8). Again, you can make "much gain" through injustice, but it is better to be just and gain only a little.

So is there a good pathway to wealth? Proverbs 13:11 says, "Dishonest money dwindles away, but whoever gathers money little by little makes it grow." In other words, you can build wealth by working hard, saving, and investing wisely. This shouldn't be shocking advice to anyone.

There are other verses in Proverbs that explain how to gain wealth in healthy, legitimate ways, but the emphasis in this book and the rest of the Bible is on how to think about wealth. You must consider the purpose of gaining wealth before you consider how. God tells us that the goal of life is to glorify him, so all other goals must support (or at least not hinder) that goal. If a goal related to making money does not fit with the more important goal of glorifying God, it is taking us in a direction away from pursuing what really matters.

Proverbs tells us to desire "neither poverty nor riches" (Proverbs 30:8). Many people claim some secret path to great riches hidden in the Bible, but God's Word actually says we should avoid wanting too much wealth. There is a fine line between wisdom that sets money aside for a rainy day and a pursuit of wealth merely for the sake of enjoying the pleasures of this world. Riches may lead our hearts away from God, who is the real treasure for us to seek (Proverbs 30:9). In addition, God is not the only thing more important than riches. For instance, "A good name is more desirable than great riches; to be esteemed is better than silver or gold" (Proverbs 22:1). Or, "A wife of noble character who can find? She is worth far more than rubies" (Proverbs 31:10).

And yet, there is wisdom in pursuing wealth in moderation. The Bible does not command us to live in poverty. "The wealth of the rich is their fortified city, but poverty is the ruin of the poor" (Proverbs 10:15). I think this means we should have enough sense to save up money so that we do not have to go into debt to pay for a sudden emergency. That requires following a budget and practicing discipline in our spending. Saving for retirement is also a standard practice for the wise, who do not want to depend on others to provide for their needs in old age.

The New Testament offers many examples of wealthy people who played a significant role in the early Christian church. Paul wrote that the wealthy members of Timothy's congregation were "not to be arrogant nor to put their hope in wealth." Instead, Paul urged them to "put their hope in God" (1 Timothy 6:17). Timothy must have had wealthy members in his congregation for Paul to give instructions about them. The Bible does not say it is wrong to be wealthy, but rather that too much wealth poses a threat to our focus on pursuing what really matters in life. The wealthy in Timothy's church were instructed to give generously to those in need in order to overcome the "root of all evil," which is "the love of money" (1 Timothy 6:10).

Proverbs gives additional instructions for those who want to gain wealth wisely, in moderation:

## 1. Spend your money on things with eternal value.

"Honor the LORD with your wealth, with the firstfruits of all your crops" (Proverbs 3:9).

## 2. Stay out of debt.

"The rich rule over the poor, and the borrower is servant to the lender" (Proverbs 22:7).

## 3. Don't spend more than a sensible budget will allow.

"He who loves pleasure will become poor; whoever loves wine and oil will never be rich" (Proverbs 21:17).

## 4. Be generous with your money.

"A stingy man is eager to get rich and is unaware that poverty awaits him" (Proverbs 28:22).

## 5. Avoid seeking to get rich quick.

Instead, have a long-term strategy for building wealth. Shortcuts will not be worth it in the long run. "Whoever gathers money little by little makes it grow" (Proverbs 13:11).

## 6. Avoid gambling and risky investments.

Instead, work hard for your wealth. "Lazy hands make for poverty, but diligent hands bring wealth" (Proverbs 10:4).

## 7. Do not measure wealth by money alone.

"Better a dry crust with peace and quiet than a house full of feasting, with strife" (Proverbs 17:1).

## 8. Do not make money at the expense of others.

For example, don't seek to win lots of money in a frivolous lawsuit or own a business that profits from promoting drunkenness. Remember, wealth must fit with the higher goal of loving God and loving others. "Better a little with righteousness than much gain with injustice" (Proverbs 16:8).

While these biblical principles and others can help you build wealth, keep in mind that even the wise use of money is no guarantee against poverty. Calamity may strike anyone, and God may even allow the righteous to go through hardships so they have something greater than financial security. Proverbs 11:28 warns, "Whoever trusts in his riches will fall, but the righteous will thrive like a green leaf." While the "righteous will thrive," that does not mean they are secure and can trust in riches. While the Bible encourages us to work toward wealth in moderation, we must never trust in wealth.

We have seen that the Bible has a lot to say about money. What about work? Your job will most likely be the main way that you contribute to your finances. But should finances be the focus of your job? First, the focus of everything should be God. Second, while finances should not be the main focus of life, we have seen from Proverbs that there is nothing wrong with pursuing wealth in moderation and with certain principles in place. So the kind of work you do should not be primarily about money, but it can certainly be a significant consideration. The Bible helps us evaluate the purpose of work by contrasting the professions of two very different people found in the New Testament.

## Herod and John

As a king, Herod had access to the finest food, clothes, and living places of his day. John the Baptist was a prophet who ate locusts, wore clothing made from camel's hair (not exactly the softest material), and lived in the wilderness. Yet, despite these disparities in wealth, the Bible portrays John as a much more successful person.

Three different times in Matthew 14, Herod is portrayed as someone controlled by others. That stands out because a king is supposed to be the one in charge. However, when Herod had John arrested, it was not because he wanted to arrest him, but "because of

Herodias, his brother Philip's wife" (Matthew 14:3). Herodias had left her husband (Herod's brother) to marry Herod. John told Herod the marriage violated God's law. Herodias wanted to silence John, and she had control over her new husband. Herod did as he was told.

Later, Herod wanted to kill John. Again, he could not do what he wanted. This time, it was because "he was afraid of the people, because they considered John a prophet" (Matthew 14:5). Finally, Herod was forced to relent to a gruesome request from his stepdaughter. Herod gave orders for John's execution against his will "because of his oaths and his dinner guests" (Matthew 14:9). Although a king, Herod seemed like a prisoner of his circumstances. His guiding principle in life was to do whatever was necessary to maintain the support of the people around him, whether it was his wife, his dinner guests, or the subjects of his kingdom.

John the Baptist, on the other hand, had a different goal in life. He sought after God's glory, no matter the cost. That is why he could call the king to repentance, even though he had no wealth or important position. No one could stop him. Even the threat of a jail sentence could not stop him because he lived for God and not to please men. While John may not have enjoyed the wealth that Herod had, he had a much more successful career.

## Success in the Workplace

The Bible tells us how to be successful in our jobs by identifying the way we can glorify God with our careers. When God created the first people, he placed them in the garden of Eden and gave them a special command: "Be fruitful and increase in number; fill the earth and subdue it. Rule over the fish in the sea and the birds in the sky and over every living creature that moves on the ground" (Genesis 1:28). God has given us the task of ruling over creation. We not only have permission but a calling to explore our world and learn how to make the best use of it. Scientific inquiry, inventions, farming, and construction are all examples of activities that carry out God's command.

The opportunity to glorify God in the workplace extends beyond religious careers like that of John the Baptist or the pastor of your church. Doctors can apply the knowledge of science to help sick people get better. Accountants can be part of a team that is necessary to run a hospital or business. Government leaders are called by God to do various tasks and need a support staff to make their work possible. High-tech companies push the boundaries of what humans can do to manipulate our environment in ways that help us achieve new heights. Our society also needs plumbers, electricians, and waste management workers for us to be able to do all the things we do. These are not just jobs that have to be done because everyone needs to make a living. Instead, they are all part of a divinely ordained task to rule over creation.

Paul wrote, "Whatever you do, work at it with all your heart, as working for the Lord, not for human masters" (Colossians 3:23). He meant that we should do a good job whether we have a boss watching us or not. We all have a boss in heaven who is watching. God is our true king, and everything we do should be in service to him. Paul's teaching here assumes that all honest work is endowed with eternal value. We should worship God with the way that we work, not simply put in time to get a paycheck.

Does it matter what kind of work we do? First, a job should benefit others in some way. Our ultimate calling to glorify God necessarily includes loving others. A job that reaps benefits from someone else's loss or someone else's sin is not something we can do if we are on the path to true success. The right path requires using the time we put into work to serve God and serve others. That doesn't mean the only jobs we can consider are at orphanages and homeless shelters. Most jobs are helpful to others. Consider just a few possibilities:

- Grocery store cashiers serve customers and play a role in helping get food from the farm to households.
- Soldiers serve their country and protect fellow citizens.
- Students learn skills to prepare to serve others in a future career.
- Truck drivers help businesses deliver products to consumers who need them.

And so on.

After verifying that you will help others, there are additional questions to ask when it comes to evaluating a job. What job opportunities are there? What jobs best match your talents and interests? Can you make more money doing something else? These are all fair questions to consider. Sometimes, you may have to do work you don't enjoy or aren't suited for in order to put food on the table. If you are in that situation, remember that your work is not a waste of time but part of your service to God.

Another issue to consider is how a potential job could impact other goals in life. The main goal of life is to glorify God, and every goal should support this goal in some way. For example, if you are married, you should have a goal to glorify God by maintaining a close relationship with your spouse. A strong marriage is an example of a supporting goal because it supports your main goal of glorifying God. If your marriage relationship will suffer because a potential job would take you away from your spouse for long periods of time, it may not be worth it, even if the pay is much better. On the other hand, higher pay might relieve stress that unpaid medical bills are putting on your relationship. Every situation is unique, but the proper assessment of deciding between your current job and a potential one must consider the impact on the main goal of glorifying God.

God has created us with different passions and abilities. He has blessed humanity in general with a desire and calling to rule over nature. As beings made in the image of God, we want to invent, build, and explore. A job gives us a specific way to be involved in the ongoing productivity of humanity and receive financial compensation for our work. The Bible says we are wise to pursue wealth in moderation, but it also warns against the dangers of riches and the inability of riches to bring real security or a meaning to life. The main goal must always remain focused on pursuing God and his glory.

─────── ⤏ **CHAPTER 10** ⤎ ───────

# PRAYER

Then Jesus told his disciples a parable to show them
that they should always pray and not give up.

—Luke 18:1

If the goal of life is to glorify God, then prayer gives us the greatest
opportunity to directly pursue our goal. Prayer is the time when
we actually have an audience with the king of the universe. Not
only that, but prayer actually changes things. Prayer can move our
powerful God into action to heal, minister to, and protect those we
lift up in prayer. Logically, prayer is the most important contributing
activity to a successful life.

However, we don't always feel the logic of the importance
of prayer. It makes sense in our heads but not as much in our
hearts, which is revealed by a lack of prayer. Truly believing in the
significance of prayer was even a struggle for Jesus's closest disciples.
They couldn't stay awake for one hour to pray for Jesus the night
he was arrested and taken away to be crucified. That was the night
when prayer was more urgently needed than any other time in
history. Why did they fail to pray? Clearly, they didn't really believe
prayer was important or could accomplish much. If that was true of
Jesus's closest disciples on a night like that, how much more will that

be true for us? We should expect to struggle to believe that prayer is the highest calling God has given us in our pursuit of success.

There is evidence everywhere that prayer does not receive proper emphasis. While I suspect many of you skipped ahead to the chapter on sex, I have no such suspicion here. Sex is more alluring than developing a successful prayer life. Commercials regularly blast the need for drugs to perk up your sex life. Rarely will you see a PG-13 or R-rated movie come out that doesn't focus significant attention on the main characters' sex lives. Everyone knows that sex sells. Prayer is quite the opposite; at least that's how it is in our culture. That's why atheists don't have to cover their children's eyes when walking by the magazine sections for fear that their children will see headlines about "powerful prayers." But if we are to take what the Bible says about prayer seriously, we have every reason to reject the perceptions of our culture.

Great athletes live for key moments in a sports season. Many players never make it to the Super Bowl or the NBA Finals. But if the opportunity arrives, they seek to make the most of it. They work hard all year long to be successful in their sport, but when the big game is on the line, they know that whatever happens in the next brief moments will define their career as successful or not. They long for those moments and play with the greatest passion when they come.

Unfortunately, followers of Jesus don't always feel the same way about prayer. Charles Spurgeon, a great nineteenth-century preacher, lamented, "How many people there are who complain that they do not enjoy prayer." Spurgeon asserted that believers often pray "because it is their duty," but they are far "from finding any pleasure in prayer."[1] Why is this? It must be that we usually don't believe that prayer is what the Bible says it is. We wonder at some level if what we are doing is really such an important moment or just a waste of time. There is a battle in the mind to see prayer for what it truly is.

## The Problem with Prayer

The problem with prayer is not really one with prayer but our perception of it. We have doubts, even if we don't consciously acknowledge them. We want to know if our prayers are actually doing any good. We have busy lives. We constantly make decisions about what to do with our time. Spending thirty minutes in prayer means that we have thirty fewer minutes to do something else. Even as a pastor, I face the constant pull to set aside prayer time to focus on more "productive" things.

The problem with prayer is that we can't accurately measure the results. We want a breakdown on a colorful chart with lines and bars that shows exactly what we get out of our time in prayer. We pray for the sick. Sometimes they get better; sometimes they do not. Even if we don't pray at all, sometimes the sick get better; sometimes they do not. Are our prayers really making any difference?

Then there is the theological problem. The Bible tells us that God knows everything, including future events. Jesus specifically says that God "knows what you need before you ask him" (Matthew 6:8). The Bible also tells us that God loves us and that "in all things God works for the good of those who love him" (Romans 8:28). If that is the case, how can my prayers ever influence God in a positive way? Doesn't he already know what is best? Doesn't he already plan to do what is best? It seems that when I pray for what is truly best, I am only asking God to do what he was already planning to do. At other times, I may pray for something that is not ultimately for the good. In that case, I would actually be asking God to do something that is not as good as what he was already planning to do.

To visualize this problem, let's say that I'm driving down the interstate in the middle of nowhere. I am almost out of gas. A sign says that the next exit is five miles away. The sign doesn't tell me if there is a gas station at the exit or not. I know that I have just enough gas left to make it five more miles before running out completely. If there is a gas station at that exit, I will avoid running out of gas. If not, then I'm doomed.

I start talking to God, asking him, "Please, let there be a gas station there." Now, does that make any sense? I am praying for a gas station to be at that exit. In reality, that gas station is either there or it isn't. Either way, what good does it do for me to pray? Even though God could, I don't believe he would instantly make a gas station appear out of thin air, including a previously non-existent adult employee to work the cash register!

Now, it is true that God could have worked in the past to ensure that a gas station would be there. He may have even done so because he knew that in the future, I would need one to be there. However, he probably wouldn't do so simply for my convenience. Why would I ever be responsible to keep gas in my car if I knew that anytime I was about to run out, God would make sure I'd get to a gas station in time? No, God would have worked in the past to ensure a gas station would be at the exit only if it was ultimately for the good, only if it fit into his plan.

But what does my praying now for a gas station to be there have to do with God's decision, which he made long ago? Didn't he already know, before I prayed, whether it would be best for a gas station to be there? Would he really leave me without a gas station simply because I failed to pray? And would he really work to ensure a gas station would be there because I prayed, even if it would be better for me to learn a valuable lesson? Would God really alter his perfect plan to accommodate my imperfect prayers?

## The Solution

How can our prayers do any good? First, prayer is about more than trying to help people with their problems. Great prayers in the Bible model praise to God (1 Kings 8:23), thanksgiving (Psalm 100), confession of sin (Daniel 9:5–6), and rejoicing (Psalm 98:4). Prayer gives us an opportunity to respond to God's kindness to us. Perhaps the way that prayer changes us is more important than any change our prayers could make on God and his actions. Prayer is more about drawing near to the presence of God than getting what we want.

Yet when we are in God's presence, he tells us to ask him for things. Paul encouraged us to pray "with all kinds of prayers and requests" (Ephesians 6:18). Jesus told us to ask God for "our daily bread" (Matthew 6:11). He also told us that asking God for things in prayer is a way that we draw near to him, comparing it to a child asking for and receiving gifts from a parent (Matthew 7:11). If asking God for things is fundamentally flawed, then all of prayer is undermined in a critical way.

The solution to this problem requires us to understand the way that God's power, knowledge of future events, and our choices work together. Remember, the Bible portrays God as having precise knowledge of future events. He even knows what would happen in the future in a different set of circumstances. He knows what free creatures will do in different scenarios, and he can act to determine which circumstances will actually take place (see chapter 5).

God already planned out the end from the beginning (Isaiah 46:10). He knows what he will do to bring about the result that he wants. Everything that God has done and will do is good because God is good, and his plans are good. Understanding history from this divine perspective is essential to understanding how we can pursue success, even through suffering (see chapter 12). It also helps us to make sense of how prayer works.

## What Happens When We Pray

Before God even created humankind, he could have decided between different policy options when it comes to prayer and its possible influences on everything else he would do. He could have determined to do everything he knows is best without paying any attention to our prayers whatsoever. That would be the most efficient option. God would always do what is best, and our prayers would have no impact whatsoever.

But God considered another option. He could make some of his choices dependent on the requests of the people he created. God knew such a system would lead to inefficiency because not all of his actions would depend directly on his perfect will. At times, he could act in a way other than what his perfect will dictates. He might act a different way because of the failure of his people to pray or because his people prayed for the wrong things.

According to the Bible, God chose to include the humans he was creating in his decision-making processes through prayer. Why would he do this? Since God is good and his plans are good, it must follow that there are benefits to his inclusion of prayers in his decisions. Those benefits must outweigh the costs of using an inefficient model of making decisions.

Consider a wealthy man raising his child. He wants his son to be just as wealthy as he is one day. There are two options he considers. The first option is the efficient one. He will simply transfer all his wealth to the son. Suppose the wealthy man knows the future. He knows that he will die when his son is thirty years old. Therefore, he simply leaves all his wealth to his son in his will. It's that simple. Now the father knows that one day, his son will have the same amount of wealth he has.

The second option he considers is more difficult. He could train his son to know how to make money. In this option, he begins by giving his son an allowance for doing different chores in the house and in the yard. He could easily hire someone else to do the work, but he wants his son to learn character and money-making skills. Later, he invests money in his son's education. Then he takes him on as an intern in his company. He makes his son start at the bottom and earn his way to a higher position. Once the son is a high-level manager, he allows him to make decisions about how to run the company. At times, he knows that his son is about to make a mistake that will cost the company money, but he lets him do it anyway. He believes that letting his son make mistakes will help him learn valuable lessons about how to run the company when the father is gone.

Now, suppose again that the father knows the future. He knows that if he were to simply make his son wealthy by leaving him a fortune in his will, the son would squander the money. He would never learn how to make money and would spend the last decades of his life in poverty.

On the other hand, the father knows that in the second option, the son will not inherit as much money. The cost of education and the costly mistakes his son will make as a manager means there will be less money to leave him in the will. However, the son will also have greater character and knowledge about how to make money. The son will go on to grow the company, and within a few years, the son will have more money than the father ever had.

In a similar way, the fact that God listens to our prayers and acts on them brings about a certain amount of inefficiency. It would be easier for us if God simply did what was best, without paying attention to our prayers. However, God knew that a system that includes prayer would have benefits that outweigh the difficulties prayer presents. Therefore, he chose to allow our prayers to influence his decisions.

The benefits may in large part have to do with his long-term plan for us. God made us in his image for a reason. God also tells us that in the future kingdom of heaven, we will have important work to do. Heaven will not be a boring retirement consisting of sitting around on clouds and strumming harps. Paul says that we will be responsible for judging angels (1 Corinthians 6:3). Jesus told a parable in which he compared our work on earth now as a test that will prepare us for our work in the future. In the end, the "faithful servants" are told, "You have been faithful with a few things; I will put you in charge of many things" (Matthew 25:21).

When it comes to prayer, it may be that God wants to include us in his decision-making process so that we share with God in his responsibilities to care for the world. This is like on-the-job training for our work in the world to come. It may also train us for future work in this life. When we pray for our needs and the needs of others, we are focused on our need for God to act and therefore on the fact that God is active in the world. We are also presuming that our prayers in some way affect what God is doing. Therefore, we view our praying as partnering with God's work. As we grow in our relationship with God, we want to pray for the things God wants. As we pray for the things God wants, we want to grow in our relationship with him.

Prayer may also help us appreciate God's work in the world and our need for him.[2] The Bible tells us that "Isaac prayed to the LORD on behalf of his wife, because she was barren; and the LORD answered him and Rebekah his wife conceived" (Genesis 25:21). Why didn't God simply allow Rebekah to conceive without Isaac praying? Why did God allow Rebekah to conceive once Isaac prayed? Perhaps it taught Isaac and Rebekah to give God the credit for the pregnancy. It reminded them that they can do nothing without God and that God listens and responds to prayer.

Although it seems trivial in comparison, I believe that even my prayer for a gas station at the next exit can make a difference. God knew that I was going to pray for it and could have responded by intervening in some way to bring about the existence of the gas station, even years before I was going to actually need it. Since I know my prayer may actually change my situation, I have reason to pray.

When God decided that he would create a world in which meaningful prayer exists, he did so to achieve clear benefits. By "meaningful" prayer, I mean prayer that could actually change God's decisions. God knew there would be costs in allowing mortal humans to influence the decisions of an infinitely wise God, but he also saw many advantages that would make it worth it, including:

- a stronger relationship with God because we recognize our need for him
- a greater appreciation for the work God does because we are more likely to recognize he is active when we are asking him to do things
- an increased desire to see the world from God's perspective because we want to partner with him in his work
- a resulting increase in our ability to do God-glorifying ministry now and in eternity[3]

Of course, God does not always answer prayers the way we want. He reserves the right to overrule our prayers and do something better than what we ask. He also acts in response to our prayers because he is able to achieve the greatest possible good this way. Even if I am praying for there to be a gas station at the next exit, I can do so believing that I am not simply going through the motions in an exercise of futility. God really could respond to my prayers. Therefore, I am encouraged to pray and talk regularly to God. Hopefully, over time, I will pray for greater and better things than a gas station as my desires conform more and more to the will of God.

## Does God Speak to Us?

In prayer, we talk to God. But can God talk to us? If God can talk to us, we will be far more successful in life if we can learn to hear his voice. On the other hand, trying to hear a voice that isn't there could lead us down a maddening path. Many Christians have struggled with doubts about their faith or their relationship with God because they can't understand why God seems to talk clearly to others but not to them.

There is good news on two fronts. First, God's voice is real. He speaks to us today. Second, we do not need to struggle to hear it. Jesus said that God speaks to us when we read the Bible. Whenever we open the Bible and read it with a teachable spirit, God will speak to us. Jesus told us that God speaks to us today through the Bible in a debate with a group of religious leaders about the resurrection of the dead. The religious leaders argued that there is no resurrection, but Jesus supported the resurrection from the Bible. He told them, "But about the resurrection of the dead—have you not read what God said to you, 'I am the God of Abraham, the God of Isaac, and the God of Jacob'? He is not the God of the dead but of the living" (Matthew 22:31–32).

"I am the God of Abraham" is a quote from Exodus 3:15. God spoke these words to Moses from a burning bush nearly fifteen hundred years before Jesus was born. The Bible gives us a record of this revelation to Moses. Yet Jesus said that when the religious leaders of his day read those words in the book of Exodus, God also spoke to them. "Have you not read what God said to you?" God originally spoke the words to Moses, but when we read them today, God also speaks to us. The Bible records God's revelation in the past, but the Bible is more than a record of his revelation to others. Through it, God reveals himself to us today. That is one reason the Bible is called "God's Word."

We do not need to hear an audible voice to hear from God. Even in biblical times, God rarely spoke this way. Neither do we have any indication from the Bible that God uses our thoughts to speak to us. There are no instructions in the Bible on how to distinguish between the thoughts rolling around in our head and the authoritative voice of God. Rather, God has sent his Spirit to dwell within us (Galatians 4:6). God's Spirit uses the words of the Bible to speak to us. The Holy Spirit can call verses of the Bible to our mind and use them to convict us of sin (John 16:8), encourage us in the faith (Romans 8:16), or guide us in the decisions we should make (John 14:26, 16:13).

The more we meditate on God's Word, the more he will speak to us. Even when we are not reading the Bible, God can lead us to recall a biblical passage or principle from his Word. God's voice is not far from us, but "very near you; it is in your mouth and in your heart so you may obey it" (Deuteronomy 30:14). God wants a relationship with us that is a two-way conversation. We speak to God through prayer, and he speaks to us through the Bible.

---

1.   Charles Spurgeon, *The Power of Prayer in a Believer's Life,* ed. Robert Hall (Lynnwood, WA: Emerald Books, 1993), 61–62.
2.   Scott W. Moore, "The Problem of Prayer" (PhD Diss., Southwestern Baptist Theological Seminary, 2006), 186.
3.   Ibid., 179–96.

---
## ⤙ CHAPTER 11 ⤚

# JOY
---

You make known to me the path of life; you will fill me with joy in your presence, with eternal pleasures at your right hand.

—Psalm 16:11

Many followers of Jesus aren't always sure what to do about joy. On the one hand, Jesus told his disciples, "Blessed are those who mourn, for they will be comforted" (Matthew 5:4). He also told them to "deny themselves and take up their cross" (Matthew 16:24). Perhaps the Christian life is supposed to be about mourning over sin and suffering in the world while denying ourselves any pleasure. We should only strive to bring joy to others. Isn't it selfish to pursue our own joy? Isn't selfishness the opposite of what we are supposed to seek as Christians?

On the other hand, the Bible commands us to pursue joy. The Psalms frequently call on us to rejoice. For instance, Psalm 100 opens with, "Shout for joy to the LORD, all the earth." Jesus explained that his instructions were given to his disciples "so that they may have the full measure of my joy within them" (John 17:13). Paul commanded us to pursue joy when he wrote, "Rejoice in the Lord always" (Phil 4:4). Clearly, God wants us to pursue joy.

But how do we do both? If we are supposed to rejoice in the

Lord always, when will we ever have time to mourn? Is it possible to have joy and mourn at the same time? Christians know that, realistically, we cannot walk around continuously with big smiles on our faces. That would be fake and dishonest.

Tension rises as we try to reconcile the need for the authentic expression of various emotions with the call to rejoice always. The result is that we often conclude that joy must have nothing to do feeling happy. Joy must be redefined to refer to something other than an emotion.

I often hear people say something like, "Happiness comes and goes but joy is something that endures." I also hear people talk about joy as if it is something you can bury deep inside and not really feel. For example, "I feel really down today, but nothing can take away my joy." I don't think either of these statements is quite right. The intention is to strip joy of its status as an emotion and turn it into something you believe, a sort of positive mind-set.

## What is Joy?

In reality, joy is an emotion related to happiness. *Merriam-Webster* defines *joy* as "the emotion evoked by well-being," "the expression or exhibition of such emotion," and "a state of happiness."[1] The original Greek word is also defined as "a state of happiness and well-being."[2] I think it is obvious that joy must be a kind of happiness that we actually feel. We don't describe others as "joyful," if there is no evidence of happiness in their lives, so why should we think of ourselves as an exception?

Joy and happiness mean essentially the same thing. However, we often separate them by context. The seriousness of the event we are experiencing affects which of the two words we typically choose to describe our feelings. Ice cream can make someone happy, while a marriage proposal may cause joy. Ice cream is something that can cheer someone up when they are having a bad day. It is a simple thing. It isn't hard to get. It doesn't last long. Most people can get ice cream just about anytime they want. It would sound odd if I told you, "Getting that ice cream filled me with joy." I might say that, but it would be unusual or an intentionally humorous exaggeration of the significance of the ice cream to me.

Meanwhile, I would not hesitate to use the word *joyful* to describe a young woman who just heard the marriage proposal she had been longing to hear for over a year. That is a rare event. Some people never get one in their entire life. It has far greater and lasting benefits than what a scoop of ice cream can offer. The young woman could replay the proposal scene in her mind years later and continue to find joy in it.

The use of the word *joy* in the context of noteworthy events leads us to think of it as something more enduring and deeper than happiness. It's not that there is something different in the emotion itself, but joy is based on more significant things. However, it would be a mistake to think that happiness comes and goes, while joy is something you can possess no matter how you feel. No, in order to have joy, you must feel happy.

So how do we rejoice always and also mourn? First, it is possible to have different emotions in reaction to the same events. If someone were to break into my house and steal everything I own, I would have a range of emotional responses. I would be both sad about what I lost and angry because of what someone did to me. I might not focus on both emotions simultaneously. I might cry tears of sorrow one moment and pound my fist in anger the next. I wouldn't really feel anger and sorrow at exactly the same moment, but if someone asked me how I was feeling, I could easily say, "Sad and angry."

I think joy and sorrow can come together in the same way. Christians are to rejoice always, even though there are times we will mourn. Even Jesus wept when his friend Lazarus died (John 11:35). While we are living in a fallen world, we mourn because of our own sin and the painful effects of sin in the world. Yet we rejoice because of the hope that we have in Jesus. Even if thieves were to steal everything I own, even as I alternately focus on feelings of sorrow and anger, I would also rejoice. I would rejoice knowing that my success in life does not ultimately depend on the security of my possessions. I would rejoice knowing that God is watching over me and would not have allowed this to happen if it wasn't ultimately for the good.

When Paul says to rejoice "always," I don't think he means that we must feel happy at all times, to the exclusion of all other emotions. I think he means that true happiness will always be present with our other emotions. Sometimes we may focus on other emotions, but we also have the ability to focus on joy. Remember that joy is different from happiness only because it is based on more significant things. What more significant thing could there be other than God loving us enough to send Jesus to die for our sins, call us his children, and give us eternal life? When we rightfully mourn over sorrowful experiences, we can and will also think about these experiences in the context of what God has done for us in Christ Jesus, and we will rejoice.

Jonathan Edwards, the famous preacher of the Great Awakening, wrote that the joy of saints is "attended with godly sorrow and mourning for sin."[3] Mourning for sin reveals that God is at work in our hearts, giving us the desire to pursue him and his ways. We mourn because God is continuing to reveal changes we need to make in our thinking and behavior so we can be prosperous and successful. Mourning for sin displays the activity of a gracious God in our lives, and that is a cause for great joy. We do not need to focus on joy and sorrow simultaneously at all times, but believers seek to have both.

## Emotions

God created us to experience emotions like joy, sorrow, and anger. In the past, many psychologists thought of emotions as something in us, beyond our control. For this reason, people will still use excuses for inappropriate anger like, "I just had to let out all this anger that was building up inside me." Or, "I can't help the way I feel." Unlike psychologists of the past, today, cognitive behavioral therapists maintain that we can control our emotions by changing the way we think and behave.[4]

Once again, modern psychology is catching up to what the Bible has always maintained about the human condition. The Bible reveals that we can control our emotions. God commands us to avoid sinful anger and also to have joy. He would not command certain emotions if it was impossible to control them. God also calls us to self-control (2 Pet. 1:6).[5] But controlling emotions does not mean that we change them directly by the sheer power of our will. Instead, we control the things that cause our emotions. Rather than impulses we have no power over, emotions are indicators of what is going on inside us. They reflect our values and beliefs. They indicate what's going on inside of us that is right and that is wrong.[6]

Think of the warning lights on the dashboard of a car. If the "Low Oil" light comes on, you may have an oil leak that has led to the oil level getting too low for your car to function properly. The problem is not the warning light; the problem is what the warning light is indicating. Someone might propose solving the problem by covering up the warning light. They could tape a piece of paper over it. But that doesn't actually solve the problem; it just silences the indicator of the problem.

God has given us emotions as indicators of what is going on inside us. Those emotions can indicate that we are doing well or that there is a problem. We can control our emotions, but not directly by trying harder to have good emotions like joy instead of bad emotions like worry. Instead, we can change our underlying thinking and behavior, which results in better emotions. Our actions are not really controlled by our emotions; rather, our emotions are controlled by our actions.[7]

Joy is a benefit and indicator of success in life. In sports, the goal of competition is to win. The goal of the season is to win the championship. When a team of athletes succeeds in attaining that goal, they feel the thrill of victory. They rejoice. The joyful emotion that accompanies victory indicates that they were successful. They didn't use practice time to work on feeling joyful all season long. They didn't develop celebration skills by practicing jumping up and down and rehearsing victory speeches. Instead, they used practice time to focus on what they needed to do to triumph in games and win a championship. They focused on physical conditioning and athletic skills. They worked on getting better at running specific plays. They focused on winning. Joy was something that came as a result of their success in becoming a championship team. Joy functioned as an indicator of a successful season.

Consider another example. What do you do when you are hungry? You desire the feeling of fullness in your stomach, so you eat food. After eating a certain amount of food, you feel satisfied. You don't obtain the feeling of satisfaction by pursuing it. You don't sit in a room without any food and meditate on trying to feel full. No, hunger leads you to pursue food, which results in satisfaction after you eat it.

In the same way, as Christians, we want joy. But we know that the path to joy is in pursuing God and his plan for our life, not the emotion itself. Joy is the indicator that we truly are on the right path. Joy is the satisfaction that we find in God alone.

I have described emotions as general indicators of how we are doing in our pursuit of success. This does not mean that someone who struggles with depression is not succeeding in life or is not pursuing God as much as someone who has feels happier. Depression is more complicated than that. As I described in chapter 4, emotional struggles can also be related to physical issues. Some will struggle with particular emotions more than others, even if they are both pursuing God the same. The presence of sin in the world means that there is brokenness all around us that can't be patched up in a simple way. However, the principles I am laying out here offer the most hope for overcoming emotional struggles.

Even secular counselors now recognize that addressing thinking and behavior is the most effective way to deal with symptoms of depression and other negative emotions. I believe that people who struggle with depression can find joy in pursuing God, even in the midst of their pain. Joshua 1:8 lays out the strategy: meditate on God's Word and put it into practice. In addition, there are common traps to avoid that can interfere with obtaining joy. Next, I will identify and address three of these joy defeaters: emotionism, legalism, and contractism. I have already begun to identify emotionism. It is pursuing the emotion of joy rather than the one in whom we will find joy.

## Avoiding Joy Defeaters

God wants us to have lives full of joy. He commands it. He designed us to find fulfillment and joy in him. Jesus said, "I have come that they may have life, and have it to the full" (John 10:10). There is nothing wrong with desiring a joy-filled life. However, this does not mean we can do it any way we like. Emotionism is one of the wrong ways to obtain joy because it makes positive emotions the highest goal of life. When joy becomes more important to us than glorifying God, we fail to obtain either. Instead, we should recognize joy as a benefit that accompanies those who are living for God. Then we pursue joy by making God's glory our top priority.[8]

The same principle is true in romantic relationships. Imagine a man who pursues a woman solely because he believes she will make him happy. He wants her to date him because it will make him feel good. He wants her to spend time with him so that he is not lonely. He wants to prove to himself and others that he is capable of getting a woman of her beauty to date him. He really has no concern for her happiness whatsoever. Such a relationship may provide him with a cheap thrill for a time, but it is nothing like a serious, committed relationship.

Alternatively, another man develops deep feelings for a woman. He wants to make her happy. He considers the activities she enjoys and takes her on dates to do those things. He is thrilled with the idea that he can bring her happiness. He marries her, raises children with her, and stays by her side to care for her when she is sick. He loves her more each year. He will find far more joy in that relationship than the first man could ever dream of. Relationships are most satisfying when we care more about the other person than ourselves. If you truly want joy in your life, don't ask, "How can I have more joy?" Ask, "How can I please God?"

## Legalism

Legalism is a second major joy defeater. We typically think of legalists as people who are sticklers for the rules and believe that they are holier than the rest of us because of it. Legalists include these people, but the problem of legalism is broader and usually more subtle.

We might also think of a legalist as someone who loves rules and laws. Actually, when it comes to God's laws, just the opposite is true. Psalm 1 tells us that a blessed person is one "whose delight is in the law of the LORD, and who meditates on his law day and night" (Psalm 1:2). The Bible encourages delight in law. Legalism is not an overexuberance in law. Legalism is actually a failure to delight in God's law.

Legalism begins with a distorted understanding of the love and graciousness of God. Legalists cannot grasp how loving God truly is. As a consequence, legalists view his law with suspicion. They do not trust that God's law is a good gift from a loving creator.[9] The law is a burden imposed on us or a test given to us so that we might prove we are worthy. Finally, the legalist accepts the challenge, "enduring" the law for the sake of some benefit. The legalist thinks, *I will follow all these burdensome laws so I can be a good person who will go to heaven one day.* The legalist may also think that keeping laws will help them earn God's favor and earthly rewards as well.

Inevitably, legalists begin to view law-keeping as a competition, and they naturally turn to see how everyone else around them is doing. They look for confirmation that they are good law-keepers by identifying evidence that they are doing better than the people around them. They often will let you know that they are doing better than you. They may focus on seemingly unimportant rules they follow well in order to gain an advantage over others in their own minds. This final stage of legalism is the most visible form, and that is why we associate the holier-than-thou attitude with legalism. But looking down on others is actually just one common effect of legalism. Legalism itself goes much deeper.

Legalism kills joy. Legalism puts up with God's law to get a future reward. Just like a youthful employee may be willing to clean toilets or do other menial tasks for the boss in the hopes of one day getting promoted to a dream job, so the legalists toils away under the law so that something better may come from God in the future. If something better does come, legalists believe they earned it. There is no joy in thinking the good things you get are only what are owed to you anyway.

Contrast this with the person "whose delight is in the law of the LORD" (Psalm 1:2). Such a person rejoices that God has given us the law. God's commands are an unearned gift. The one who delights in the law does not see the law as something to endure in order to earn something else. Rather, the law itself is something to delight in, for it guides us in pursuing God. It tells us how to love like God and live the way he designed us to live.

The blessed person of Psalm 1 receives the law gladly and with a grateful heart. Such a response to the law has no motive to evaluate everyone else's law-keeping. They aren't trying to win a competition with others but are simply pursuing God. The best way to overcome legalism is to keep looking to the cross and remember how loving the God who gave us the commandments truly is and how undeserving we are. As our confidence in God's love grows, our legalistic view of God's law will fade away.

## Contractism

Contractism is closely related to legalism. Contractists expect to receive something in return for living the Christian life and are offended when the appropriate compensation doesn't come in. They view "carefully doing everything written" (Joshua 1:8) as their part of a contract-like arrangement and a pain-free life as the part of the contract God is obligated to do as a result. They say things like, "I've faithfully attended church all these years, so why am I not able to get pregnant?" Or, "I served God all during high school. I was active in my church and stayed out of trouble. But I was turned down from all the colleges I applied to."

Contractists have fallen into the legalist trap, because they think Christian teachings are a burden to endure, rather than a gift to delight in. They also commit the emotionist fallacy, because they are not pursuing God but rather what they can get from God. They don't ask, "How can I please God?" but instead, "What do I have to do to get God to please me?" God isn't someone to delight in but a means to another goal. The other goal has become a higher priority than God. When God doesn't deliver, disappointment sets in.

Contractism is really a modern version of idolatry. Ancient people believed that the gods had different powers, but one thing they could not do was get their own food. The only way a god could eat was to have people present food before an idol representing it in a temple. The one offering food through idol worship was doing the god an important favor. In return, the people believed the god was now obligated to use its particular power to bless the one making the offering, which could mean fertility, rain, or protection. Temple offerings were a way of entering into a contract with a god to receive certain benefits. There was no other reason to serve them.[10] The contractists of today think of the one true God in the same way. They offer obedience to God's commands and expect something in return.

The contractist mind-set pops up frequently, even among mature believers. It is an attitude we must guard against. The Bible gives many examples as a warning to us. For example, Job's friends come to comfort him and give him advice in the midst of the great suffering he was going through. His sons and daughters died, he was financially ruined, and he was stricken with painful sores all over his body. "Surely," they told Job, "all this must be because of some great sin you have committed." Exasperated, Job responded with statements like, "How long will you torment me and crush me with words?" (Job 19:2).

The story of Job reveals something we have known all along. Sometimes, terrible things happen to the best people. God does not limit the experience of suffering to those who are especially wicked. Jesus added that the reverse is also true: The wicked are often treated better than they deserve. The Father "causes his sun to rise on the evil and the good, and sends rain on the righteous and the unrighteous" (Matthew 5:45). There is no evidence in the Bible that God offers a contract where he promises that earthly circumstances will directly correspond to our behavior.

God is a gracious and loving God. However, he has not set up the world to give us perfect and immediate compensation for everything we do, whether good or bad. Our good deeds are not bargaining chips to get favorable treatment from him. Job found this out, and we will examine his story more in the following chapter on suffering.

In reality, there is something God offers that is better than "favorable" treatment from him: God himself. The psalmist declares, "Take delight in the LORD, and he will give you the desires of your heart" (Psalm 37:4). When you make God the goal of your life, he will not disappoint. Don't pursue God's law to get a better life or protection from hardship. Instead, pursue God's law because God's law is good. Consider who gave it to us. The psalmist also wrote, "With my lips I recount all the laws that come from your mouth. I rejoice in following your statutes as one rejoices in great riches" (Psalm 119:13–14).

1.   Merriam-Webster, "Joy." accessed January 29, 2019. https://www.merriam-webster.com/dictionary/joy.
2.   Frederick W. Danker, Walter Bauer, William F. Arndt, and F. Wilbur Gingrish, *A Greek-English Lexicon of the New Testament and other Early Christian Literature* (Chicago: University of Chicago Press, 2000), 1074.
3.   Jonathan Edwards, *Religious Affections* (Goodyear, AZ: Diggory Press, 2007), 180.
4.   Judith S. Beck, *Cognitive Behavior Therapy* 2nd ed. (Guilford, New York, 2011), 30.
5.   Brian S. Borgman, *Feelings and Faith* (Wheaton: Crossway, 2009), 64–65.
6.   Ibid., 26.

7. Jay E. Adams, *Competent to Counsel* (Grand Rapids, MI: Zondervan, 1970), 94–97.

8. John Piper, *Desiring God* (Colorado Springs: Multnomah, 2003), 294–95.

9. Sinclair B Ferguson, *The Whole Christ* (Wheaton: Crossway, 2016), 88–95.

10. Douglas K. Stuart, *Exodus*, The New American Commentary (Nashville: B&H, 2006), 450–51.

———— ❧ **CHAPTER 12** ❧ ————

# Suffering

Consider it pure joy, my brothers and sisters,
whenever you face trials of many kinds.

—James 1:2

Facing "trials of many kinds" does not sound like a cause for "pure joy." Is it possible to rejoice in unemployment, a cancer diagnosis, or the loss of a loved one? James isn't suggesting that it is merely possible to rejoice despite our suffering. Nor is he telling us to focus on our blessings when we suffer and rejoice in those. No, he is commanding us to always consider suffering as an occasion for rejoicing. What James says is almost certainly the most counterintuitive statement in the Bible. At first, it seems to make as much sense as a new diet plan that claims that the secret to losing weight is to eat as many doughnuts as possible.

However, there are good reasons to take what James says here seriously. First, we have a strong motive to want him to be right. If we could somehow find a way to rejoice in suffering, nothing could stop us from having a life full of joy. Of course, we would rather have joy without any suffering, but we know that is not an option. Jesus told his disciples, "In this world you will have trouble" (John 16:33). So trouble will come, but think about how much better life would be if trouble was a source of joy rather than misery. Even our greatest tragedies would be an occasion for rejoicing. So we should at least hear what James has to say about this, if only because of how much we want him to be right.

But the clearest reason to take the command seriously is the source in which it is found. The Bible has proven to be a credible book. We have already examined the evidence that it is God's Word, and God does not lie. So if God calls on us to consider it pure joy whenever we face trials, it must be possible to do so. This is not pie-in-the-sky teaching from some quack. This is James writing under the guidance of the Holy Spirit.

I also do not think James is saying that rejoicing in suffering is easy. He has not lost touch with reality. James issues the command to consider trials a source of joy in a context that recognizes the difficulty of the task. Without a doubt, it is more difficult to pursue success through suffering than in any other area in life. Remember that following Jesus often requires doing hard things that lead to life getting easier, while doing what is easy often leads to life getting harder. In chapter 1, I compared pursuing success to running in the right direction in soccer. It is easy to go the wrong way because the defenders will leave you alone. It is harder to go the right way, but it is worth it. There is simply no reason to play soccer if you aren't even trying to score a goal.

When you pursue joy in trials, you are heading in the right direction in life. The defenders will come against you and try to kick the ball away. They will make it more difficult to keep going the right way than ever before. Not all defenders are the same, and it seems that the closer players get to the opposing team's goal, the more urgent the defense will be to stop them. The other team places their toughest defenders closest to the goal. None is more challenging to get around than the goalie, who is allowed to use his or her hands. Pursuing success through suffering is like going the right direction when closest to the goal.

Pursuing success in relationships, sex, work, and prayer comes with great challenges. Pursuing success in suffering is on another level. I think learning how to be successful in the other areas prepares you to take on this greatest challenge. A quarterback never starts in the Super Bowl in the very first game of his career. Instead, he builds toward it. He plays in scrimmages and in various games in high school and college. He plays in many games in the NFL, always with an eye on one day playing in the big game. Each phase of his career prepares him for the big stage. In pursuing success in life, suffering is the big game. Pursuing success in suffering will require combining all the earlier skills covered in this book, but with the right work and preparation, you can do it.

## A Matter of Perspective

Suppose you are diagnosed with cancer. You begin treatment, and each month, you experience an increasingly unimaginable amount of pain. After a year, you die. From a worldly perspective, there is nothing good about this whatsoever. By worldly, I mean the absence of any spiritual reality. "Worldly" means looking at the physical world and the human life span as if that is all there is. From this point of view, there is nowhere to go and nothing to do after this life. Once you die, that is it.

Worldly is also a perspective that leaves God out of the equation. If there is no God, there is no personal being who has a plan and reason for why we are here. We are just here, alone in a vast, cold universe. Atheists may create meaning for their lives, but it has no objective basis in reality. From their perspective, even the artificial purpose they have created for themselves ceases at death. There is nothing beyond the here and now.

If that were the case, suffering would always be terrible. Life would essentially be a game where the goal is to get as much pleasure for yourself as possible. "Eat, drink, and be merry" (Luke 12:19). In this game, there are winners and losers. If you experience the pleasures this world has to offer and only a small amount of suffering, you win. If you get a prolonged disease and die, you are one of the losers. That's all there is to it. The goal of life is to maximize pleasure and minimize suffering.

All of us start off life with a worldly perspective. We want to be fed, nurtured, and loved. We can't think seriously about anything beyond the here and now. As we grow older, we consider a spiritual perspective at some point. However, the world's way of thinking about life continues to surround us. It pressures us into thinking that the worldly way of viewing suffering is the only one that makes any sense. When we read a passage that says we should consider it pure joy when we face trials, it sounds crazy. From a worldly perspective, it is.

But James did not tell us to consider trials a joy from a worldly perspective. He assumed a biblical view of God and our purpose for living. James saw intriguing possibilities for a positive role for suffering from the biblical view. In the verse immediately following his shocking call to rejoice in trials, James continued, "because you know that the testing of your faith produces perseverance" (James 1:3).

In this short explanation, James introduced two important principles for considering trials pure joy. First, he identified trials as a "testing of your faith." Trials are tests of our faith because they challenge us to see things from a spiritual perspective rather than a worldly one. Second, James indicated that the cause of rejoicing in trials is not the pain from suffering, but the benefits the suffering produces (in this case, perseverance). Let's look at these one at a time.

## A Faith Perspective

I believe that James calls trials a "testing of your faith" because faith includes seeing God at the center of all of life. A trial challenges us to hold onto faith. A trial can lead us to ask, "Where is God now?" Whenever we suffer, we face temptation to abandon the biblical view of life in favor of the worldly one. A strong faith will pass the test by rejoicing in trials, while a weak faith will fall short. Our response to suffering will cut through our claims and perception about our faith and show how strong it really is.

Faith is a central theme in the book of James. Statements like "faith without works is dead" (James 2:26 KJV) help us understand what he meant by the word *faith*. Today, a popular understanding of faith is that it means something like "believing something is true even though there is a lack of evidence." A person might say, "I've just got to have faith in God," in much the same way they would say, "I've just got to have faith that my team is going to pull out the victory" (even though they are currently losing by a wide margin). However, neither James nor any other biblical authors used the word *faith* this way.

Instead, the Bible always portrays faith as accepting the evidence, even when it is hard. I have faith that God exists because I do not see any other reasonable explanation as to why the world is the way it is (see chapter 2). I have faith that God is good and in control because the Bible reveals that this is so, and the evidence supports the truthfulness of the Bible. I would have to reject evidence and reason to not have faith in the goodness of God. There is no such thing as blind faith in the Bible.

But faith is also more than simply nodding in agreement that a statement is factually true. Faith results in acting a different way. That is why James said "faith without works is dead," meaning that a faith that makes no difference in the way you act isn't actually faith at all.

In addition, biblical faith is not a force in and of itself. I can't make something happen through my faith. Instead, faith is a belief in something. Biblical faith is a confidence in the good activity of God, even when he is not plainly visible. A person with faith acknowledges that God's power and goodness are real, with serious implications for the way to live life. Faith doesn't change circumstances, but faith will impact how to view and respond to circumstances.

So faith is based on evidence and impacts how we act and how we think about life. Yet, in the midst of suffering, faith is not easy. What do we do when we know we have reason for faith but are struggling to keep it? Joseph is a great example of someone who had faith in the goodness of God (see chapter 5), even when it was difficult. He had faith that God was actively doing something in all the suffering he experienced when his brothers sold him into slavery.

As a result, Joseph kept working diligently to serve God wherever he was, both as a slave and when he was sent to prison after being falsely accused. If Joseph did not have faith, he would have responded with laziness and bitterness. He could have reasoned to himself, "Why should I work hard for my master? I shouldn't even be here. It's not fair." But faith led him to a different response.

That doesn't mean it was easy for Joseph. James would say that he experienced a testing of his faith. Joseph had reason to have faith that God was involved in his suffering for a good purpose. He knew about what God had done for his father, Jacob. He also knew about God's promises for him through the dreams he received. It must have been difficult for him to keep acting according to that knowledge. But the way he acted revealed a strong faith.

Like Joseph, every one of us has sufficient reason to have faith in God. The Bible gives us a reliable testimony to the truth of God's power and goodness. God tells us in his Word that "our light and momentary troubles are achieving for us an eternal glory that far outweighs them all" (2 Corinthians 4:17). God has a good and satisfactory reason for every trouble we go through, even if we don't know what it is. We have a legitimate reason to pursue success through suffering.[1]

For thirteen years, Joseph had no idea how all the pain in his life would be for the good. But he kept living with faith that it was for the good. He served God faithfully wherever the Lord placed him, with no evidence of bitterness in his heart. After years in prison, he was suddenly called up to explain a dream to Pharaoh that indicated a severe famine was coming on the whole region. Pharaoh elevated him to a position of administration over the entire nation. Joseph was able to provide food for his starving family.

God used these events to grow and shape the newly forming nation of Israel. He used Israel to bring about the Messiah, the savior of the world. God used his knowledge of what would happen in different circumstances and activated a glorious plan. Joseph eventually saw all the good that came out of his suffering. Usually, we do not know the good that will come from our suffering.

Sometimes, we never find out what the good is in this lifetime. However, we have sufficient reason to believe that there will be good, good that makes our suffering worth it. Like Joseph, we exercise faith when we have a confident expectation of the good that will come out of suffering based on the promises of God, and we act accordingly. Joseph passed the testing of his faith.

## The Cause for Rejoicing

The good news is that the testing of our faith does not merely reveal the condition of our faith. It produces something. In fact, James said that the reason we should consider it pure joy when we face trials is "because you know that the testing of your faith produces perseverance" (James 1:3). The cause of our rejoicing when we face trials is not in the suffering itself, but in what the suffering produces.[2] James did not say to rejoice in suffering because the suffering is wonderful. No, he told us to rejoice because of what God will accomplish through the suffering.

One example of what God produces through "trials of many kinds" is perseverance. A trial is an opportunity to exercise our faith. It helps our faith grow strong. Our ability to endure hardships with confidence that God is doing something keeps growing. Of course, God may accomplish many other things through our trials. However, those things may remain completely unknown to us for a long time. One thing we can know about our trials right away is that they have the potential to help us grow spiritually. Whenever we are suffering, we should stop to consider what lessons God may want to teach us through our suffering.

The Bible also promises that the testing of our faith will never exceed our ability to pass the test. Paul wrote, "No temptation has overtaken you except what is common to mankind. And God is faithful; he will not let you be tempted beyond what you can bear. But when you are tempted, he will also provide a way out so that you can endure it" (1 Corinthians 10:13).

## Paul's Example

Paul also emphasized the remarkable ability Christians have to rejoice in suffering. He wrote to the Philippians, "I can do all things through him who strengthens me" (Philippians 4:13 NASB). When he said, "all things," he did not mean he could fly to the moon or win ten straight Super Bowls. The verse has nothing to do with physical strength. Paul was specifically talking about rejoicing in all things, including suffering.

Paul was going through a trial himself. He wrote the letter to the Philippians during a long period in prison. He was awaiting a trial he knew could result in the death penalty. Like Joseph, Paul continued in his faith that God was doing something good through his suffering. He explained, "Now I want you to know, brothers and sisters, that what has happened to me has actually served to advance the Gospel. As a result, it has become clear throughout the whole palace guard and to everyone else that I am in chains for Christ" (Philippians 1:12–13).

Paul was the greatest missionary who ever lived. His work of establishing churches and spreading the Gospel throughout the Roman world makes him arguably the most accomplished Gospel minister in history. He could have easily questioned why God would allow him to be shut away in prison for years. "God, I need to be out doing your work rather than sitting here in chains; why don't you do something?" But Paul did not complain that way. He saw ministry opportunities in the prison, and he knew that was exactly where God wanted him. He had faith that God knew what was best.

So in that context, he could write, "Rejoice in the Lord always. I will say it again: Rejoice!" (Philippians 4:4). Then he identified the secret to rejoicing always, even in trials. He continued, "I know what it is to be in need, and I know what it is to have plenty. I have learned the secret of being content in any and every situation, whether well fed or hungry, whether living in plenty or in want" (Philippians 4:12). The secret is to trust that God is active and is accomplishing something good through every situation. When you have faith in that, you can "do all things," meaning you can rejoice in the Lord in every circumstance.

Paul also described the secret in Romans 8:28: "And we know that in all things God works for the good of those who love him, who have been called according to his purpose." We know that Paul meant that the good that comes from suffering will be greater than the suffering itself (see chapter 5). However, we must be cautious to identify the kind of good Paul is talking about here. Paul is not saying that a trial will necessarily produce a greater good from a worldly perspective. For example, he does not mean that if you get laid off from your job, you will soon get a better job, or if the college you applied to turns you down, there must be a more prestigious college that is going to accept you.

Sometimes, our worldly circumstances can improve as a result of our suffering. Joseph was elevated to the second most powerful position over all Egypt as a result of the trial he went through. However, I highly doubt that he would say all the suffering he endured was worth it, if it was only for a powerful position. Like Joseph, Paul was spending time in prison because of injustice. Paul rejoiced while in prison, but not because he thought some better position was coming, nor did he ever get one. There was a different kind of good that led Paul to rejoice in his suffering. He never asked, "How will God use my suffering to create better circumstances for me?" and neither should we.

Perhaps the good Paul had in mind is spiritual growth. We could connect Romans 8:28 with the concept in James that the testing of our faith "produces perseverance." Paul does go on to say, "For those God foreknew he also predestined to be conformed to the image of his Son" (Romans 8:29). The "for" connects Romans 8:29 with the preceding verse, the promise that God works for the good in all things. One of the things God does through our suffering is help us to grow to be more like Christ in our attitudes and actions. Like James, Paul called us to consider how God may use suffering in our life to help us become more like Jesus.

However, the potential for spiritual growth does not fully explain how God works all things for the good. Consider the suffering of people who do not believe in Jesus. God may use that to help them come to faith in Christ, but many do not. Their suffering does not help them grow spiritually. When their suffering includes their death, it is impossible to see how they could personally benefit in a way that would be worth it to them. I believe God uses their suffering for the overall good, but that good may not actually benefit the person suffering.

In Philippians, Paul did not identify the good that came from his suffering with his spiritual growth. It's possible that he grew spiritually from his suffering in prison, but we have no indication that the spiritual benefit alone outweighed the pain he endured. Instead, Paul specifically connected the good that came from his suffering with the advancing of the Gospel (Philippians 1:12). The good wasn't something that benefited Paul but rather the Gospel. In fact, our suffering does not usually bring about a greater good for us personally on earth.

Does this mean that we sometimes have nothing to gain from our suffering? I think it comes back to perspective. Your view of God actually determines whether your suffering is worth it to you or not. Notice that Romans 8:28 contains a significant qualification. The verse does not promise that "in all things, God works for the good of all people." No, the verse says the promise is only "for the good of those who love him." It says this promise is for those who love God, those "who have been called according to his purpose." There is something about the good that God accomplishes in suffering that is valued more by those who love him than by those who don't. The good outweighs the suffering for those who love God, but that is not necessarily so for those who don't.

The qualification "those who love him" identifies those who are on God's team. Imagine a star basketball player having an amazing game, hitting one basket after another, grabbing rebounds, and finally, hitting the game-winning three at the buzzer to win the championship game. You would celebrate this player's performance, if you are on the winning team. If you are not, it would not be a good outcome for you.

For a real-life example, consider Judas. After he betrayed Jesus, he regretted his actions. He was suffering under the guilt of what was going to happen to Jesus and the knowledge that he played a significant role in having him put to death. Could God work it all for the good? Yes, absolutely. The Crucifixion of Jesus led to the salvation of all those who put their faith in him. God accomplished a greater good through the wicked actions of Judas, the religious leaders, and Pilate.

However, the Crucifixion did not work for the good of Judas personally. Jesus referred to Judas as "the one doomed to destruction" (John 17:12). Judas never truly repented for his actions. He felt really bad because of what he did, but he never sought God's forgiveness. Instead, he tried to end the pain he felt on his own terms; he took his own life. The Gospel accounts about Judas reveal that he was never a true disciple of Jesus but was taking advantage of his position as treasurer by helping himself to the disciples' money (John 12:6). He is an example of someone who lacked "Godly sorrow ... that leads to salvation and leaves no regret." Instead, he had "worldly sorrow" that brings death (2 Corinthians 7:10).

The tragedy of the Crucifixion had no benefit to Judas. He did not meet the qualification of one who loves God. God did work the Crucifixion for the good, just not for the good of Judas. But for all who love God, the death of Jesus was for the good. God always works things for the good from his perspective, to accomplish his good purposes. If you love God, you will celebrate the good that comes from him accomplishing his purposes. What is good for God will be good for you, if you love him. If you don't, then the good that God accomplishes may not be worth it to you personally.

The fact that our suffering may not directly benefit us should not disappoint us. If we have the right goal in life and view suffering through faith, we will rejoice in the good that comes from our sufferings. Paul rejoiced in his sufferings because he knew God was achieving greater glory by advancing the Gospel. Since Paul's goal in life was glorifying God, he knew that his suffering was helping him achieve what was most important to him.

## Pursuing Success through Suffering

God always accomplishes his glory through suffering. Therefore, everyone who has "been called according to his purpose" (Romans 8:28) has a good reason to pursue success through suffering. Notice that I said *through* suffering. I do not mean merely that we should pursue success even though we are suffering or despite our suffering. Instead, we are to view suffering as a unique opportunity for success. Remember, God will accomplish something through our suffering that is greater and more than worth the suffering we are going through. One principle we can derive from this concept is that the greater the suffering, the greater the good that will come from it. The more you appear to lose, the more you know you will gain.

For the sake of illustration, let's put this in purely monetary terms. Imagine that you have a sum of money magically deposited to your checking account every time you lost money. Whenever you have a certain amount of money stolen or have to pay an unexpected expense, twice that amount of money appears in your account by the next week. If that were the case, you would celebrate losing money. If somebody picked your pocket and took two hundred dollars in cash, you would be excited because you know that four hundred dollars is coming your way. The more money you lost, the more excited you would be.

Now, of course, the good God brings about is not tied to dollar amounts. However, the good does outweigh the bad, nonetheless. If I have two hundred dollars stolen, I know that the good that will come out of it will be something more valuable than that amount of money (but probably not money). The more I lose, the more I can rejoice.

What is it that I gain? First and foremost, I know that God is accomplishing his purposes, even though I may not know what they are. It may not even benefit me personally from a worldly perspective, but it will be for the glory of God. Since my life's purpose is to glorify God, I can celebrate, knowing that I am achieving something through my suffering that is helping me succeed in the most important goal in life. Something is happening that has eternal value and is worth pursuing.

Suffering presents us with the greatest opportunity to glorify God. Anyone can praise God when all is well, but a prayer of praise to God in the midst of suffering carries a special significance. The story of Job tells us this. Satan was sure that Job only served God because of all the blessings he had given him. Satan used Job to challenge God directly: "Stretch out your hand," Satan urged, "and strike everything he has, and he will surely curse you to your face" (Job 1:11).

However, even after devastating loss, Job "got up and tore his robe and shaved his head. Then he fell to the ground in worship" (Job 1:20). Later, he told his wife, "Shall we accept good from God, and not trouble?" (Job 2:10). Job faced immense suffering. However, God was glorified through his response to that suffering. Job's suffering was temporary. But for all eternity, Job knows that his faithfulness led to God's defeat of Satan's accusations. That is something no one can ever take away from him.

One of the themes of the book of Revelation is that God's people will utterly defeat Satan through their willingness to suffer and remain faithful to God. Through enduring great persecution, they will glorify him. John wrote, "They triumphed over him by the blood of the Lamb and by the word of their testimony; they did not love their lives so much as to shrink from death" (Revelation 12:11). We can celebrate all suffering because through it we have an opportunity like no other to fulfill our life's purpose.

In addition to glorifying God through suffering, we should always consider how the pain we are going through might benefit us spiritually. We should ask, "What can I learn from this experience?" "How might God use this pain to conform me 'to the image of his Son'?" (Romans 8:29). If we don't focus our attention on questions like these, we might miss an opportunity to fully obtain a blessing God has for us.

In my own battles with suffering, I have found that the deepest times of pain are when I have drawn closest to God and have found the most joy in his presence. Whenever I am living life relatively free from suffering, I can easily begin to trust in the things of this world to provide security and happiness. But when I experience loss, I have a heightened realization of how transitory and ultimately meaningless the things of this world are. I am reminded that no matter what happens to me in this life, my security is found in a heavenly Father who loves me more than anyone else. That's when a proper perspective on God and his role in my life returns, and I rejoice. Although it is natural to think that suffering is an enemy of joy, through Christ Jesus, "I can do all things through him who strengthens me" (Philippians 4:13 NASB). I can consider it pure joy when I face trials of many kinds.

---

1. Jay Adams, *How to Handle Trouble* (Phillipsburg, NJ: P&R Publishing, 1982), 18–25.
2. Ibid., 39.

# CONCLUSION

Have I not commanded you? Be strong and courageous.
Do not be afraid; do not be discouraged, for the LORD
your God will be with you wherever you go.

—Joshua 1:9

God did not tell Joshua to sit back and let success come his way. He called Joshua to take action: "Keep this Book of the Law always on your lips; meditate on it day and night, so that you may be careful to do everything written in it. Then you will be prosperous and successful" (Joshua 1:8). In the next verse, God urged Joshua to pursue success with boldness. He told Joshua he could do so without fear, based on the assurance that he would be with Joshua "wherever you go." The promise of God's continuing presence also extends to all followers of Jesus.

After teaching his disciples the commandments, Jesus called them to action. Just as Joshua 1:8 promises blessings for carefully doing what is written in the Book of the Law, so Jesus told his disciples, "Now that you know these things, you will be blessed if you do them" (John 13:17). Like Joshua 1:9, he then told his disciples not to be afraid: "Do not let your hearts be troubled" (John 14:1). He also assured them of his presence: "Surely I am with you always" (Matthew 28:20). The Bible also promises that "God sent the Spirit of his Son into our hearts" (Galatians 4:6).

God's continuing presence in our lives should encourage us to pursue success with boldness. There is nothing we need to achieve success that God will not provide. Remember, Jesus once fed five thousand with two loaves of bread and five small fish, with plenty of food left over. Jesus can certainly provide what you need to be prosperous and successful.

Remember, God did not promise to do everything for Joshua; he promised to be with him. God called Joshua to work hard. Like Joshua, God has called us to continually meditate on the teachings of the Bible while seeking to put them into practice. James put it this way: "Whoever looks intently into the perfect law that gives freedom, and continues in it—not forgetting what they have heard, but doing it—they will be blessed in what they do" (James 1:25).

In other words, if you are going to benefit from the Joshua 1:8 promise in your life, you have to take action and do what the verse calls on you to do, with the full assurance that God will be with you "wherever you go." You have to meditate on the words of the Bible and carefully do them. This calls for a significant commitment, and I have done my best throughout this book to demonstrate that making the commitment is worth it. I want to conclude with some practical help on what to do next.

In order to meditate on God's Word, day and night, you must first start reading it regularly. You need to make plans to do this; it will not just happen. Decide when you will make time to read the Bible, and stick to it. Pick a time that works for you. There are many Bible apps you can download in order to always have the Bible with you on your phone. You may want to consider an audio Bible.[1] I also recommend Bible reading plans that give a reading assignment for each day. They help me stay accountable to where I am supposed to be in my reading.

Another important component is Bible memory. The two most common responses I hear to Bible memory are, "Is it really that important?" and "I can't do that." First, I do think it is that important. When I memorize Bible verses, I understand them much better. I am able to pay attention to the details of a verse that I don't normally notice by reading once or twice. Over time, as I review verses, I think of new ways that the verses apply to my changing circumstances. Having a list of memorized verses also helps me make connections between different parts of the Bible. I meditate on the Bible at a deeper level when I read a passage and think, "This verse reminds me of one of my memory verses; I wonder how they are related?"

As to the second objection, "I can't do that," let me assure you that you can. Remember, God will be with you. Bible memory requires some time and a good amount of dedication, but you can do it, and it is worth it. Choose verses to memorize that challenge the way you think about God or that address an area in your life you need to work on. For example, you could start by memorizing Joshua 1:8.

Break the verse down into phrases. Read the first phrase multiple times. Then say it multiple times without looking at it until you know you it well. Then work on the second phrase. Next, work on saying the first two phrases together. For Joshua 1:8, begin with "Keep this Book of the Law always on your lips." Read it and reread it until you can say it comfortably from memory. Then add, "meditate on it day and night." You can memorize any passage by working on one phrase at a time.[2] Next, review the verse the following day. After a few days, you will only need to review the verse each week, then each month. After a few months, the verse will be firmly planted in your long-term memory. If you need help getting organized, I highly recommend getting an app for your phone.[3] You can also write your verses down on a set of index cards.

In addition to reading and memorizing, you will need to commit to studying the Bible. By this, I mean you need to develop your understanding of the background to the Bible and consider many possible ways of interpretation. The more you know about the authors, time periods, and languages of the Bible, the more accurate your understanding of the text will be. When you only interpret the Bible by yourself from a twenty-first-century Western context, you are bound to make mistakes. How can you evaluate which interpretation better fits the text if you haven't even heard of interpretations other than your own? Bible study seeks to expand your ability to evaluate biblical texts from different perspectives.[4]

Bible study can take place privately or in a small group setting. I enjoy studying the Bible with a small group of people because someone will almost always notice an insight in the text that I skipped right over. People who have had different cultural backgrounds or experiences will look at a text from an angle I wouldn't naturally consider. For example, a friend who recently discovered her spouse was having an affair might look at the story of David and Bathsheba in a different light than a single person or someone who has never gone through that painful experience. My understanding of the text may grow when I hear what my friend has to say about it.

In private study, you can also benefit from the insights of others. A good study Bible with book introductions and notes on individual verses can help you grow in your understanding of the Bible while you read regularly. Read other commentaries or books on theology when you can. I have heard some people criticize spending time on books about the Bible. "Read the Bible, not books about the Bible," they say. I agree that the Bible should be our primary focus, but we need the collective wisdom of others who have studied longer and have considered a wide range of interpretations in order to grow in our understanding of the Bible. Reading the Bible alone will not help you if you do not make progress in understanding what you are reading.

Of course, meditating on the Bible is not the only requirement to be prosperous and successful; you must do what it says. Let me recommend that you don't merely think to yourself, *Yes, I will try to do what it says.* Instead, identify one thing you will start doing, and do it. Perhaps there was one chapter in the second part of this book that you realize needs more attention than others. If so, go back through that chapter and identify one action step. Determine a specific time and place you can begin to put that step into practice, and do it. If you are struggling with a specific problem and need more guidance to come up with a biblical approach for addressing it, see if there is a biblical counselor in your area.[5] Biblical counselors are trained to help people find biblical solutions to life's problems.

## Day and Night?

If you are not used to regular Bible reading, memorization, and study, this may sound overwhelming. It almost sounds like you become obsessed with the Bible. Even so, does it really match the "day and night" qualification of Joshua 1:8?

I believe meditating on God's Word day and night is about a lifestyle of thinking about God's Word. It doesn't mean you never think about anything else or never sleep. It means that growing in your understanding of the Bible is an ongoing project and the top priority on your to-do list. It requires set times for study, but more than that, it requires a mental attentiveness to biblical thinking throughout the day.

I do not think it is a sin to go a day without reading your Bible. You may have a day or two each week that is particularly busy when you don't get to your Bible reading. But are you thinking about new biblical insights from the previous day's reading? Are you thinking about what the Bible says about different situations you encounter each day? That is far more important than having a perfect record in Bible reading every day. It is possible to read the Bible for twenty minutes every single morning and never think about the Bible during the rest of the day.

Although the word *obsessed* has a negative connotation of overdoing it, we do need to have a love for God's Word that many in the world would think of as an obsession. Consider what God instructed the Israelites when he first gave them the Book of the Law. He told them, "These commandments that I give you today are to be on your hearts. Impress them on your children. Talk about them when you sit at home and when you walk along the road, when you lie down and when you get up. Tie them as symbols on your hands and bind them on your foreheads. Write them on the doorframes of your houses and on your gates" (Deuteronomy 6:6–9).

God called the Israelites to talk about the Bible throughout the day. They were told to wear visible reminders of the commands on their body and on their buildings. Jews to this day practice these commands literally. The Israelites also had one day in seven to cease from their regular work and focus on God, as well as many days throughout the annual calendar to reflect on God's redemptive acts throughout history. God knows that his people need to be immersed in the Word to have success putting it into practice.

I think we would do well to surround ourselves with music, jewelry, posters, regular Bible study times, and anything else that will help us focus on God's Word. Church is also an important part of immersing ourselves in biblical instruction. Through church, we can connect with small groups for studying the Bible. Churches give us the opportunity to meet for worship with other believers at least once a week. Churches also help us follow an annual calendar full of reminders of biblical events such as the birth of Christ and the resurrection. Biblical preaching develops our understanding of the Bible and its proper interpretation. God has used preaching throughout biblical times and in church history to call his people to action in response to the Bible. No wonder the author of Hebrews wrote, "Let us consider how we may spur one another on toward love and good deeds, not giving up meeting together" (Hebrews 10:24–25).

If all this sounds like an obsession, so be it. God says that it is the key to being prosperous and successful. I don't think there is anything wrong with an obsession for pursuing success God's way. This may sound overwhelming, but remember: God is with you. Take it one step at a time. Begin developing a lifestyle of meditating on God's Word. Be strong and courageous. I will close with this prayer for you that was first offered by Paul for the Christians in Ephesus:

"I pray that you, being rooted and established in love, may have power, together with all the saints, to grasp how wide and long and high and deep is the love of Christ, and to know this love that surpasses knowledge—that you may be filled to the measure of all the fullness of God" (Ephesians 3:17–19).

1. I recommend the audio Bible app, *Dwell,* https://dwellapp.io/ (subscription required) and for Bible reading, *YouVersion,* https://www.youversion.com/.

2. For more help with Bible memory, see Andrew Davis, *An Approach to Extended Memorization of Scripture* (Greenville, SC: Ambassador International, 2014).

3. I recommend *The Bible Memory App,* https://biblememory.com/. The app will help you select, categorize, and memorize verses. Then reminds you when it is time to review each verse.

4. I believe neglecting a Jewish perspective on the Scriptures has been the greatest mistake Christians have made in interpreting the Bible correctly. The Bible was written either entirely or almost entirely by Jews, and their theological perspectives have largely been ignored or misunderstood. In order to see the Bible from a Jewish perspective, I highly recommend the study materials from First Fruits of Zion, https://www.ffoz.org/.

5. The Biblical Counseling Coalition lists a number of different places to look for a biblical counselor at "Find a Biblical Counselor," https://www.biblicalcounselingcoalition.org/find-a-biblical-counselor/.

# SELECTED BIBLIOGRAPHY

Adams, Jay E. *Competent to Counsel*. Grand Rapids, MI: Zondervan, 1970.

___. *How to Handle Trouble*. Phillipsburg, NJ: P&R Publishing, 1982.

___. *A Theology of Christian Counseling*. Grand Rapids, MI: Zondervan, 1979.

Beck, Judith S. *Cognitive Behavior Therapy*. 2nd ed. New York: The Guilford Press, 2011.

Borgman, Brian S. *Feelings and Faith*. Wheaton, IL: Crossway, 2009.

Copan, Paul. *When God Goes to Starbucks*. Grand Rapids, MI: Baker, 2008.

Cowan, Steven B., and Terry L. Wilder, eds. *In Defense of the Bible*. Nashville: Broadman & Holman, 2013.

Davies, Paul. *The Cosmic Jackpot*. New York: Houghton Mifflin, 2007.

Davis, Andrew. *An Approach to Extended Memorization of Scripture*. Greenville, SC: Ambassador International, 2014.

DeYoung, Kevin. *Just Do Something.* Chicago: Moody, 2009.

Dorsey, David A. *The Literary Structure of the Old Testament.* Grand Rapids, MI: Baker Academic, 1999.

Edwards, Jonathan. *Religious Affections.* Goodyear, AZ: Diggory Press, 2007.

Ehrman, Bart D. *Did Jesus Exist?* New York: Harper One, 2012.

Ferguson, Sinclair B. *The Whole Christ.* Wheaton, IL: Crossway, 2016.

Geisler, Norman, and Frank Turek. *I Don't Have Enough Faith to Be an Atheist.* Wheaton, IL: Crossway, 2004.

Geisler, Norman, and Thomas Howe. *When Critics Ask.* Grand Rapids, MI: Baker, 1992.

Gudgel, David. *Before You Live Together.* Ventura, CA: Regal, 2003.

Hawking, Stephen. *The Illustrated A Brief History of Time.* New York: Bantam, 1996.

Heiser, Michael S. *The Unseen Realm.* Bellingham, WA: Lexham, 2015.

Hodges, Charles D. *Good Mood Bad Mood.* Wapwallopen, PA: Shepherd Press, 2012.

Jacobs, A. J. *The Year of Living Biblically.* New York: Simon & Schuster, 2007.

Keathley, Kenneth. *Salvation and Sovereignty.* Nashville: Broadman & Holman, 2010.

Kinnaman, David, and Gabe Lyons. *Good Faith*. Grand Rapids, MI: Baker, 2016.

Komoszewski, J. Ed, M. James Sawyer, and Daniel B. Wallace. *Reinventing Jesus*. Grand Rapids, MI: Kregel, 2006.

Lambert, Heath. *A Theology of Biblical Counseling*. Grand Rapids, MI: Zondervan, 2016.

Leiter, Charles. *Justification and Regeneration*. Muscle Shoals, AL: HeartCry Resources, 2007.

Lewis, C. S. *Mere Christianity*. Nashville: Broadman & Holman, 1996.

Moore, Scott W. "The Problem of Prayer." PhD Diss. Southwestern Baptist Theological Seminary, 2006.

Moreland, J. P., and William Lane Craig. *Philosophical Foundations for a Christian Worldview*. Downers Grove, IL: IVP Academic, 2003.

Noble, Alan. *Disruptive Witness*. Downers Grove, IL: InterVarsity, 2018.

Piper, John. *Desiring God*. Colorado Springs: Multnomah, 2003.

____. *Don't Waste Your Life*. Wheaton, IL: Crossway, 2003.

Reeves, Michael. *Delighting in the Trinity*. Downers Grove, IL: InterVarsity, 2012.

Ross, Hugh. *The Creator and the Cosmos*, 3rd ed. Colorado Springs: NavPress, 2001.

Sande, Ken. *The Peacemaker.* Grand Rapids, MI: Baker, 2004.

Spurgeon, Charles. *The Power of Prayer in a Believer's Life.* Edited by Robert Hall. Lynwood, WA: Emerald Books, 1993.

Strobel, Lee. *The Case for Christ.* Grand Rapids, MI: Zondervan, 1998.

Wallace, J. Warner. *Cold-Case Christianity.* Colorado Springs: David C. Cook, 2013.